Jefferson Davis

The life of Jefferson Davis, President of the Confederacy, is a dramatic story of a frustrated man. In this absorbing biography the distinguished critic and historian Allen Tate balances the story of Davis with that of the Civil War into which he reluctantly led his people. Several times the South appeared close to winning the war. Several times, too, President Davis misjudged the capacity of both friend and foe. Mr. Tate analyzes the character of the South as well as of Davis in his account of a great American crisis.

LIVES TO

REMEMBER

JEFFERSON
DAVIS

by

Allen Tate

G. P. PUTNAM'S SONS NEW YORK

Contents

Jefferson Davis

1 The Man and the Hour

THE MORNING of January 21, 1861, was, in Washington, D.C., cold but fair, so that by eleven thirty the carriages rapidly approaching the Capitol along Pennsylvania Avenue were splattered a little less than usual with the village mud of the "City of Magnificent Distances." On the sidewalks, from Willard's Hotel near the Treasury, on down past the National Hotel, and thence to the Capitol itself, little knots of people gathered, quickly dispersed, formed into other knots of people. It had been a month and a day since the secession of South Carolina. Excitement was high; the common business of the hour went undone. And in the last twelve days, four more states had left the Union. Most of the local population, being Southern, openly rejoiced, for the doddering and neutral President was obviously, out of sheer bewilderment, going to let the seceding states have their way. To the Republicans, who were held at bay until March 4, President James Buchanan's indecision was little bettter than treason; to the Southerners, who had put him in office, it was downright bad faith.

Traitor was now beyond doubt the role of Senator Jefferson Davis from Mississippi. His state had been, on January 9, the next after South Carolina to go out of the Union, and still be remained in Washington and, because the news had not been official, kept his seat in the United States Senate. He had, said hostile rumors, led a conspiracy of Senators from the Lower South to overturn the government; for such was the Republican gloss upon the document called "To Our Constitutents," drawn up, signed, and forwarded by these Senators to their respective states. The paper announced that relief must be found in secession and then in the organization of a Southern Confederacy. It had been sent out early in December, as the signal to South Carolina to secede. Davis, moreover, on the day after Mississippi's declaration of independence, had addressed the Senate on affairs in South Carolina, defending her position and denouncing the vacillation of the President. Republican Senator Lyman Trumbull had risen to agree with the Senator from Mississippi that the President was at fault—but, of course, for a different reason. He had then charged the Senator with the possession of secret information of the intentions of the government toward the forts in Charleston Harbor. Davis, he intimated, was staying in Washington as long as possible to spy and to conspire, to lobby as many

10

other states into treason as he could, and to paralyze the action of Buchanan until the South was united.

For more than a month, Davis had been ill. He was not able to travel. Besides, he had no specific duties to perform in Mississippi; he had been called to none. Moreover, he thought he might, by a miracle, bring the fire-eaters of both sides to their senses. It is true that he had, in November, just after Abraham Lincoln's election, written to Robert Barnwell Rhett, Jr., the editor of the Charleston *Mercury,* that "if the secession of South Carolina should be followed by an attempt to coerce her back into the Union, that act of usurpation, folly, and wickedness, would enlist every true Southern man for the defense." But he had warned Rhett against hasty action in South Carolina. Davis was cautious and hesitating and was not, in the phrase of the times, a secessionist per se.

The events of the following month therefore become exceedingly remarkable. After all explanation is done, they remain mysterious to this day. For Davis, the ablest debater for Southern rights since John C. Calhoun, was, for reasons that we shall see, emotionally bound to the Union.

Between January 12 and 21, Davis was still suffering from dyspepsia and neuralgia, and he was confined to his house. Governor Francis Pickens had asked him to come to South Carolina, but on the eighteenth Davis told him that his presence was suddenly needed in Mississippi, that he did not have time to come to Charleston at all. He had been appointed to the major generalcy of the Army of Mississippi, and on the morning of the twenty-first he went to the Senate for the first time in eleven days, to say farewell.

The news that Davis would speak had preceded him; the Senate was full, only a few seats, those of already departed Southerners, being empty. In the gallery, inconspicuous and looking straight ahead, sat Mrs. Jefferson Davis. In a moment her husband would rise.

He rose. For a few seconds he hesitated, standing perfectly erect, almost swaybacked, in the manner of statesmen and other great men of his time. A stranger, unmoved by the scene, might have wondered what kind of man he was. He was not tall, but he looked tall, because he was slender; he was faultlessly dressed in black broadcloth, wore a black silk handkerchief tied stockwise around his neck and a white stiff shirt and black satin waistcoat. His long brown hair fell on either side of a high, square, finely modeled forehead; beneath heavy brows, deep-set gray eyes looked out with a kind of unseeing intensity; a handsome aquiline nose, perfectly set in his face, almost hid a mobile, receding upper lip. Under the high cheekbones lay deep hollows; these and the square jaw and protruding chin gave the whole face a look of extreme emaciation—and of an iron will. A glance at this man would have revealed his possession of absolute self-mastery. Looked at more closely, he might have seemed less harmonized than self-conquered, as if he had suppressed a certain instability of temperament by will alone and then ignored it.

12

This man, whom William Seward later called the brains of the "Secession Plot," without whom the "plot" could not have succeeded, had actually made himself ill in the last four or five months trying to avert secession. His warning to the younger Rhett was only an incident in his efforts toward that end. While back in 1850 he had tried to bring the South to break up the old Union, doubts and misgivings had come upon him; he had changed his mind. In 1850 secession might have moved on unopposed. The North was less powerful than in 1860; the Middle West had filled up with new immigrants; the population there was still largely Southern in sympathy and interest. But the Nashville Convention of 1850, dominated by Robert Barnwell Rhett, Sr., and by William Lowndes Yancey and Davis, had not been able to get behind it a united South.

The Compromise of 1850 and Stephen Douglas' success with popular sovereignty in the Kansas fight seemed to prove the secessionists to have been wrong. Rhett, the John the Baptist of the movement, for whom Davis was later to be the very unsatisfactory messiah, was now discredited. In 1850 the people did not want to secede; the Compromise and popular sovereignty, both apparently successful, told them that they did not need to. Davis had shared the optimism of the South over the popular sovereignty issue; but when it was clear that the South could not hold its own in Kansas, that the "slave empire," so eager to expand, was not sufficiently eager to fill up the territory with Negroes and obtain a majority, Davis knew that Douglas, out of self-interest, had betrayed the interests of the South. Douglas, the wiliest demagogue of the time, knew that the North would win Kansas and he the Northern vote; by appearing to give the South an equal chance he expected to win the Southern vote, too. Davis at last saw through Douglas' tricks and became his enemy. This enmity was in a few years to become the immediate cause of secession, though Davis, a poor analyst of events, saw this too late.

At Charleston, in 1860, the Democratic Convention would not nominate Douglas, and Douglas was the only candidate the Northern Democrats would vote for. Davis and Yancey defeated him, because he had betrayed the South, but they defeated him only to elect Abraham Lincoln. In the summer of 1860 Davis saw his error and asked Douglas to withdraw his independent candidacy in favor of a candidate whom both sections might unite on. Then Douglas shrewdly, and for once honestly, replied that he was the only man the Northern Democrats would vote for. By failing to nominate Douglas, Davis and Yancey had split the Democratic Party, the only national power left in the country equal to holding the sections together.

Davis could not lead Mississippi into secession in 1850; by helping to ensure the election of Lincoln, he unwittingly forced his state to secede, and now nothing he could do would prevent it.

The "Secession Plot" had evidently gone beyond the original plotters, for the conspirators were a whole people. If Davis had been a secessionist in 1850, he had not even then been a secessionist of the Rhett school. He belonged with Calhoun, who was committed to preserving the rights, even the supremacy, of the South within the Federal Union up to the last moment. The elder Rhett, that profound and cynical statesman, saw that all compromise with the North was futile, that the South must come to secession or, in the end, to gradual domination by the North.

Before Jefferson Davis began to speak, he looked around at the vast audience with a kind of sad gravity. Even as he stood, the crowd noiselessly increased; ladies sat on the floor in the aisles, or with their bright colors checkered the sofas in the passageway in back of the Senate forum; the reporters' gallery held the entire diplomatic corps. Davis' glance withdrew reluctantly from the crowd, as if he dreaded to speak. Then in a voice that faltered over the first words, but gathered in volumes as he went on, he began:

I rise, Mr. President, for the purpose of announcing to the Senate that I have satisfactory evidence that the State of Mississippi, by a solemn ordinance of her people in convention assembled, has declared her separation from the United States. Under these circumstances, of course, my functions terminate here. It has seemed to me proper, however, that I should appear in the Senate to announce that fact to my associates, and I will say but very little more. . . . It is known to Senators who have served with me here, that I have for many years advocated, as an essential attribute of State sovereignty, the right of a State to secede from the Union . . . If I had thought that Mississippi was acting without sufficient provocation . . . I should still, under my theory of Government, because of my allegiance to the State of which I am a citizen, have been bound by her action. . . . Mr. President, and Senators, having made the announcement which the occasion seemed to me to require, it remains only for me to bid you a final adieu.

Davis sat down, but the audience, as if it expected more or was not satisfied with the formal simplicity of his words, waited an instant before it burst into deafening applause. His head in his hands, he shrank from the ovation; there were whispers in remote corners that he was weeping.

The farewell was one of the most characteristic speeches Davis ever delivered; it betrayed the curious separation of his intellect and his feelings. Beneath the beautifully coherent defense of the secessionists ran a note of regret for what he was about to leave behind. It was something more than the loss of the habits of fifteen years, though these, for a rigid character, must have been hard to break; it came down, in the end, to an emotional timidity, a fear of changing the objects of one's attachment, a kind of inertia that no amount of intellectual conviction could quite remove. He was emotionally undeveloped, and for this reason he could not altogether get at the motives of men.

The theory of states' rights and the belief in secession had been equally understood in both sections when advantage dictated understanding. As late as 1846 the state government of Massachusetts had been willing to secede and had passed resolutions to that end, in opposition to the Mexican War. The North alone now repudiated state sovereignty, because it had no interest to serve with its support. But Davis never quite understood that conflicts are not decided by citations of the law or by the results of discussion. The intellectual habits of the secluded, theoretical student had not been altered by his years in politics; they had been transformed into the habits of the parliamentary committeeman. Not even the events of December had taught him the implacable motives of the North.

After the Republican Senators had rejected the Crittenden Compromise, which would have given to them every eventual advantage and, to the South, nothing in the end, they would not listen to a proposal of the Southern states. They were then challenged for a compromise proposal of their own, but not a Republican replied.

At this distance it appears certain that the deadlock exactly suited the North, for its purpose was to subdue the South at all costs; in a policy that conceded nothing and demanded everything, the North meant to "ride over the South roughshod." The South at this time was willing to accept any measure that guaranteed it even less than its Constitutional rights in the territories, but the North no longer desired equality of sectional power; the North was bent upon domination. By refusing to budge from this position, the North forced the South to act for its preservation, and by means of the slavery issue, the shrewdness of the Yankee succeeded, as always, in putting his enemy in the wrong.

There was probably not a single phase of this conflict that Davis failed, in a sense, to understand; yet, in the end, he could not see why men would not follow the law or why the inflamed sections would not abide by compromises. Men sometimes act reasonably, but almost never logically. This was a distinction that Davis, being logical, could not grasp.

If it is true that Davis, the secessionist, wept at the end of his farewell to the Senate, it is remarkable that his opponents, who denied the right to secede, shed not a tear. For there were only two parties in America that knew their own minds and the minds of each other. The Republicans were determined to hold and dominate the South, and they had no reservations that unsettled their purpose. The extreme secessionists understood this purpose and were equally determined to get away before it was too late.

Lincoln, on the other hand, meant to hold the South, but not to dominate it, and thus his idea of the Union was unique and grand; it was mystical and almost religious, and it later became the rationalization of the motives of the North in a war of conquest. Lincoln is one of the few characters in history whose real greatness it was found convenient to use; his sublime character and the motives of the North became identified.

Lincoln and the war became the same thing, but they were very different. The sole idea of Lincoln to be realized was the geographical Union, and he is actually the most defeated great man in American history.

The most completely vindicated is the little-known Robert Barnwell Rhett, Jr., the prophet of secession, who, from the dingy office of the Charleston *Mercury,* had thundered against half measures in the South for more than twenty years. The South was destroyed, and the American nation became what he said it would become. He saw the weakness of the Southern faith in mere political action—its futility against the extralegal procedure of the North, whose most clamorous and radical leaders were driven by irrational, fixed ideas that recognized no Constitutional authority whatever. The slow, temporizing Southern intelligence could not cope with such a force, for which the body politic was no longer a reality. In the industrialized North, government and men as political entities were instrumental to the superior ends of commerce and trade.

Davis was the last of the Senate giants. He was a giant ridden by dyspepsia and neurasthenia, morbidly sensitive and emotionally undisciplined, his emotional instability bulwarked behind a boundless intellectual pride. He lacked emotional resilience, and he could not read the meaning of events. He could cap the hour with a formula; he could analyze the theoretical significance of the passing moment, for he had done this for ten years in the Senate, with a logical acumen that held spellbound even his enemies. He could shatter the arguments of his shrewdest opponents, but he could not fathom the opponent's political cunning or forestall its success. He always won over Douglas in debate, but Douglas won the political battle in the end. Davis could not feel his way into the future or foretell the results of his own decisions. He was therefore constantly surprised—and constantly disappointed. He could not see why a beautifully arranged program should not succeed. Davis' powerful will could not make up for a lack of emotional conviction, and he was doomed to the obstinate support of half measures and, by his lack of vision, to the mere hope that it would all work out well in the end.

In 1861 the capital of Alabama was a large town radiating from one street, a mile long, that ran from the beautiful Alabama River gently upward to the capitol, white-columned and classical in the early spring sun. For years the cotton trade in Montgomery had been falling off, and now the main business was government; neither streets nor houses had about them that look of bright impermanence which is the sign of hurry and trade. The town bore an air of solid dilapidation that would never quite topple into decay, an air of changeless repose.

At the moment, however, there seemed to be a quickened and unusual pulse in the life of the town. Near the capitol the crowd was gathering quickly. The day was February 4, 1861. The galleries of the senate hall of the Alabama legislature were packed. Below, grave and deliberate, as if they had been there forever, sat the thirty-eight delegates to the Constitutional Convention of the Confederate States of America.

As a collection of portraits, their like will not be seen again in American history, for, had they but known it, they were there to enact their own extinction, to write the obituary to their race. This distinct Southern type, developed in the Lower South, had produced a unique philosophy of action that bears no name. Outside political forms it was inarticulate; for nearly forty years it had been put on the defensive by the anti-slavery agitation; it could not afford the leisure and detachment that the development of a highly conscious, deeply realized literature requires.

The makers of the Confederate Government were political and not philosophical minds. Not one of them was individually so original as the society that had brought him there; the new impulse of that society was to be frustrated, because its leaders could think only in politics—the politics of the United States Constitution. Because that document had been their best defense within the old Union, they imagined it to be the government best suited to a new social order, and they were wrong.

Above the rest, Howell Cobb, the presiding officer, formerly Secretary of the United States Treasury, surveyed the convention with an air of utter casualness, as if new nations were formed every day and it was nothing to get excited about. Cobb's drooping eyes, a little puffy, his long hair and full beard, joined in an

21

expression mixed of quizzical cunning and innocence. He was master of a town of more than 1,000 Negroes, one of the largest slaveholders in the South.

One man had come only to write the new Constitution, and he succeeded in doing it. It took him five days. But it was less the genius of the Honorable Alexander H. Shephens than his determination, and still less the genius of the assembly at large, which brought into existence a new nation in so short a time. Possibly the Southern aptitude for parliamentary tactics had something to do with it. The real explanation is the political inertia that pervaded the convention, the poverty of ideas, the deep-seated reluctance of the delegates to part with the old Union. Torn between Sodom and salvation, the delegates prepared only for compromise with the Washington Government—to be rid of Washington and yet to keep it. There was no determined leadership in the opposite direction; no leader rose who saw the inevitable war, and the Confederacy was hobbled from the start by an intricate system built on the assumption of peace.

Stephens was the only man of conviction who had influence with the Federal Government because he had fought secession in Georgia to the last hour. He was a confirmed Unionist, won to the Confederacy only by technical allegiance to his state.

He was the most remarkable-looking figure of his age. Little more than five feet tall, he weighed about ninety pounds and had the body of a fourteen-year-old boy. At a glance he looked hardly older than that.

But the almost beardless face was seamed with fine wrinkles, and the small slits of eyes, dull and lightless, were the eyes of a nonagenarian. He was a lifelong dyspeptic, and he looked too frail to outlive the moment, but the stunted frame was driven relentlessly by a powerful will and by an acute, one-track intellect.

He was not unlike Davis. The Constitution that Stephens gave to a hesitating Confereracy exhibited no lack of formal ingenuity, but it was mainly a critical revision of the old Constitution from the Southern viewpoint; it was theoretical and, in view of the desperate crisis, unimaginative. It assumed that the Southern Government would be let alone, permitted to conduct a high-minded debating society. It reverted to the Articles of Confederation for an explicit statement of the sovereignty of the states, but it declared, nevertheless, that the Confederacy was permanent. It prohibited all duties for the protection of industry. The President's term was to be six years; he could not succeed himself. Cabinet officers could speak on the floor of Congress. The slave trade was abolished forever. The Confederate Constitution was, no doubt, in many respects superior, looked at from eternity, to the Constitution of the United States. A New York newspaper admired it extravagantly, urging it as the basis of sectional reconciliation. With unconscious irony, it divined the purposes of the Montgomery Convention.

The new government was provisional. The Constitution had to be ratified; the permanent order would not come in for a year. It might then be too late to take the drastic measures that the situation required. The members of the convention could not believe that the South had to win its independence, and there were no extraordinary provisions to that end. To conciliate the lukewarmists, they had been put in power, and a strong policy was sacrificed to the appearance of harmony all around. Robert Toombs and Cobb had won the secession of Georgia against Stephens and Benjamin Hill; Toombs was cast aside and Cobb given the safe honor of the presiding chair. Rhett, in the midst of a crisis that he, more than any other man, had helped to make, was suspect and powerless. The fate of secession was in the hands of those who did not want it.

It was now February 9. The Constitution of the Southern utopia having been made, Howell Cobb casually, almost indifferently, rapped for order.

He said, "The next business of the Convention is the election of a provisional President of the Confederate States."

Each state had one vote, and there were six votes in all: South Carolina, Georgia, Alabama, Mississippi, Florida, Louisiana. Tellers were appointed by the chair to collect and count the votes. They were J. L. M. Curry of Alabama and William Porcher Miles of South Carolina. The result was foregone, but when the tellers had gathered the six slips of paper and read them, they approached the chair and whispered the name to Mr. Cobb.

He rose and, with great deliberation, said, "It is my

24

duty to announce that the Honorable Jefferson Davis of Mississippi has been unanimously elected provisional President of the Confederate States of North America." Stephens was elected Vice-President.

The mystery of the election of Jefferson Davis, who was not even on the scene and who had done nothing whatever in his own behalf, is still unsolved. There are three possible explanations of it. He was, in the first place, as we have seen, a reluctant secessionist, and his leadership would presumably conciliate the timid and the weak. And then, too, he had been the most powerful debater in the United States Senate, the successor to John C. Calhoun in the defense of Southern rights. Last of all—and this reason forms the sole claim to the sense of reality that the convention had—Davis was a trained soldier, and his knowledge of war might conceivably be useful—if not now, then at some not far distant time.

Davis was a graduate of West Point; he had fought in the Black Hawk War; he had commanded the First Mississippi Volunteers in the Mexican War—with such sensational gallantry that he was still popularly esteemed as a great soldier. He had been Secretary of War under President Franklin Pierce, and he was now, by appointment of Governor Edmund Pettus, major general of the Mississippi troops. He seemed to combine the qualities of statesmanship and war better than anybody else. And yet he was a dark horse, chosen because the convention had not the courage to put forth a convinced leader of the movement that it was supposed to stand for.

It was two months before Virginia would secede, and yet she was already dictating to the secession convention. She would have none of Rhett and none of William Lowndes Yancey of Alabama, the most powerful popular agitator in the South. Yancey, no less than Rhett, deserved the now somewhat quaint honor of bringing the South to what a Southern Unionist called a pretty kettle of fish. Ceaselessly and relentlessly, he had exerted all the arts of oratory.

The election of Davis involved the least risk. However, he was elected less for his experience in politics and war than for the simple fact that there was nothing against him. He was a born compromiser of ideas; what the convention did not know was that he was incapable of compromise with men. He was too proud, too sensitive to reproof; he rose, in crises, to great heights of disinterested feeling and responsibility, but, being a chronic neurotic, the price he paid was a continuous headache. As if one dyspeptic were not enough, Alexander H. Stephens was added for good measure!

It had been exactly a week since Mr. Cobb had announced the election of Jefferson Davis; it was now Saturday, February 16, 1861. The crowds seemed that day thicker than ever and the excitement greater, for Davis would be there at almost any moment.

That night he came from the railroad station into the long avenue lit by bonfires, driven in a handsome carriage, cheered by the crowd. The procession—in a moment it became that—moved slowly to the old Exchange Hotel, near the capitol, where the great men of the South waited in the glare of torches to receive him. Davis stood on the gallery of the hotel at the side of William Lowndes Yancey—Yancey, small, undistinguished-looking, in ill-fitting clothes; Davis, erect, graceful, immaculate, austere. Yancey raised his head to the crowd; silence fell. Then, with indescribable grace, the small man moved one hand toward Davis and said in ringing yet perfectly modulated tones, "The man and the hour have met."

2 King Cotton

The COTTON KINGDOM, as it was called even before 1850, covered as much as 400,000 square miles if we include all the land on which cotton could be grown at a profit. It was, in the main, a fertile, alluvial soil, washed by a network of navigable rivers, which furnished transportation from even the smallest towns to New Orleans, Charleston, and other cotton markets. Not all the land—notably not the pine barrens of South Carolina, Georgia, Alabama, and Louisiana—was suitable for raising cotton, but even these sections, with the exception of the remote mountain fastnesses, contributed, as we shall see, to the rising power and prestige of the planter. The soil, on the whole, was marvelously productive. It was too loose and open for the culture of wheat, but corn could be raised as easily as cotton. The greatest asset of the country, however, was its climate. The settler making his way down the

29

river on the "spring rise" knew that he was in no danger of starvation. Having settled in some well-watered valley, he could raise two, sometimes even three, crops of peas, potatoes, beans, and corn before the winter set in.

The land was easily acquired, too. West of South Carolina it was sold at government sales at a dollar an acre. Some settlers, however, simply "squatted" on their land, without going through the formality of a purchase.

The migration to the Lower South differed from the earlier migrations into Kentucky, Illinois, and the other prairie lands. The majority of the people were not driven from their former homes by lack of land or hard times; they were impelled by their desire to get on in the world. Many people from New Jersey, Rhode Island, and some of the New England states settled in the Lower South because they saw an opportunity of getting rich quickly. Certain other factors determined for many the goal of their migration. In Virginia, for instance, the greatest wealth was in slaves, but there was no growing demand for tobacco—always the money crop of that section—and there was no employment for hundreds of slaves. The owners of these slaves had either to sell their slaves or to move. Kentucky was no longer the promised land. Slaves could not be held in the fertile plains of Indiana and Illinois. To these gentlemen, the Lower South offered the most desirable haven, for the slaves who had been an embarrassment in Virginia could become the foundation of future wealth. They bought broad acres at ridiculously low prices, erected many-columned white mansions on river bluffs or headlands, and kept a state which, in Virginia, was no longer possible except for the very rich.

A large percentage of the planter class was made up also of people from Kentucky, Maryland, and Virginia, who were ambitious for social advancement. Social strata in the older sections were already well-established. A man, unless possessed of great personal distinction—and this in Virginia often meant merely education—was likely to remain all his life in the class in which he had been born. In the Lower South everybody was "on the make." The profits from one year's crop were often enough to set a man up as a planter and to set him up in style. The term "cotton snobs" came into vogue.

The Lower South, which has been sentimentalized over more than any other section of the country as the last stronghold of chivalry and the abode of true romance, is thus seen to have been largely a society of the newly rich. But, like the newly rich everywhere, they speedily took on the customs and manners of the local high society. The master of a plantation numbering as many as 1,000 acres lived in state and dispensed hospitality on the grand scale. In summer he went to Pass Christian on the Gulf coast or perhaps to Virginia for protracted visits to relatives. Most of the winters he spent in New Orleans, which at this time offered the most brilliant social season on the continent. Always in touch with Paris, it was the first American city to present opera; Charleston, Mobile, and Memphis were not far behind in their appreciative interest in the arts.

Only a small minority of the population of the Lower South lived the easy life of the planter. The small farmer dwelled usually in a log house, which rarely numbered more than two rooms. Sometimes it was what is known as a double cabin, with a passage open at both ends dividing the two rooms. In such a house, Jefferson Davis was born.

If the farmer prospered, he made a hall of the passage and added porches front and rear or even raised a second story. Most of the household activities went on in the large bedroom in which the farmer and his wife and youngest children slept. The cooking was done before the huge open fireplace. The family dinner, consisting of bacon, corn bread, mush, and molasses, was spread on a checkered tablecloth or sometimes on the bare boards of the pine table which stood in the center of the room. The farmer's wife washed her clothes out of doors, heating the water in an enormous pot over a fire made of chips or the smaller sticks of wood from the woodpile. If the farmer owned a Negro family, as was frequently the case, the mistress minded the young Negroes along with her own children in order that their mother might be released for service in the field.

A small farmer, like Samuel Davis, worked, as a

rule, side by side with his slaves. One such farmer boasted that he hoed row for row with his Negroes. Critics of the slave economy have pointed out that this system may have retarded his advancement considerably. It was generally said that a Negro could not or would not work as fast as a white man. The produce from these small farms was carried by wagon to the nearest plantation town, where it was exchanged for the few articles that it was necessary in those days to buy: coffee, sugar, molasses, or a bit of finery for the womenfolk.

Over in the piney woods lived still another class of people—squatters, most of them—whose right to their barren wastelands was not likely to be disputed by acquisitive planter or Federal agent. Their dwellings were rarely as comfortable or sanitary as those of the plantations slaves. They consisted usually of one-room cabins in which whole families slept on filthy beds of straw. The cabins were seldom provided with floors; trash or straw scattered on the earth was the only carpet they were ever likely to know. A few gaunt razorback hogs ranging the woods furnished salt pork in winter; a straggling patch of corn, the meal that was indispensable in the houses of rich and poor. For the most part, these people lived on fish and game.

The opulence and expansive ease of the planter, his summers at Pass Christian or the Greenbrier White Sulphur Springs, his winters at New Orleans and Charleston, his magnificent hospitality, all had been made possible by the labor of a swarm of English, Spanish, Portuguese, and New England slave traders, who for a century and a half had landed cargoes of Negroes in New Orleans or on the coasts of Virginia, Georgia, and the Carolinas.

The west coast of Africa and the areas back of it were the major field of the slaver trader's pious operations, but almost every tribe, even in the remote interior, was represented among the Negroes whose way was found for them to the shores of America.

The ultimate responsibility for slavery, of course, rests upon the native operators, who drove their fellow Negroes in herds to the coast, where they went to the highest white bidded. The white men branded and shackled their purchases and crowded them into tween decks so low that they could not stand erect through the whole voyage—often a period of months—much as chickens and ducks are pressed into crates for the market. Comfort was expensive, because space was valuable. But time was valuable, too, for if the voyage was long, the cargo might be lost through disease. The Negroes, wallowing in their own ordure, contracted infectious diseases that often wiped them out and the crew with them. The slave trader had to be endowed with a certain mixture of courage and brutality.

On reaching America, he occasionaly sold his cargo wholesale, but more often the sale was retail through factors who acted as brokers at the ports. The new Negroes, when they arrived at the plantation, were distributed among the old slaves, who taught them the language and ways of this strange land. The new hand was allowed three years for "seasoning," but sometimes he took longer to get used to his new home and to be of use to his master. Some never became acclimatized, and many died after a few months of the bloody flux or other diseases to which custom had made the old Negroes more or less immune.

The 2,000,000 or more descendants of those who survived transplanting were, by 1850, widely scattered and their tribal differences amalgamated almost beyond recognition. They had no memory of their own country except a few broken words, which oddly checker the white man's vocabulary to this day. These 2,000,000 Negroes were the foundation of the Cotton Kingdom, "the cornerstone of our new edifice," as Alexander H. Stephens called them in 1861, in a speech that was highly unphilosophical.

They lived, a conscript army of labor, in groups of cabins called the quarters, usually located near the big plantation house. The cabins, according to the scale of rural living, were comfortable; their sanitation was systematically looked after by the master. The daily ration of the Negro was a quart of corn meal, half a pound of salt pork, and a litttle molasses, with smaller portions for the children. This diet he supplemented with peas, greens, sweet potatoes, rice, and any other "garden sass" that he was able to raise in the plot of ground almost invariably allotted to him. Many slaves were permitted to raise a little nankeen cotton for their own profit; it was a brown variety easily distinguished from the master's staple kinds, a little of which otherwise the Negro might conceivably have stolen to augment his crop. The master brought the Negro's nankeen every year at the current price.

On every plantation a hierarchy of rank, privilege, and esteem was rigidly observed. The Negro man, who had behind him the longest record of faithful service was the head of the tribe and his wife the foster mother of all the other Negroes. The plantation "doctoress," who included midwifery in her accomplishments, was a high personage honored by both white and black. One doctoress boasted that she had not lost a case in two years, and the number of comfortable superannuates on the larger plantations attests to the thoroughness of the medical care that the masters provided for their Negroes. Physicians were regularly employed to make visits to the Negroes.

One, when something went wrong on Jefferson Davis' Brierfield plantation, the master asked his Negro overseer, James Pemberton, how it had happened. James answered, "I rather think, sir, through my neglect." James was a remarkable man, but there were thousands like him. Almost every family could boast of a servant as honest, as faithful, and as intelligent as James.

The sufferings of the Negro came, as a rule, in the hands of the trader, on the way to a new master. There are, in the annals of the Lower South, records of whippings, fetters, pursuits by bloodhounds, even death after flagrant disobedience.

To do the migrating planters justice, however, they did all they could to keep families together—notably during the great trek from Virginia to the Lower South after 1800. The master carried with him, beside his family and his own slaves, all the broadwives—that is, wives owned abroad on neighboring plantations—whose masters could be induced to part with them. The despotism, but for rare exceptions, was benevolent, for it was to the planter's interest, aside from a matter of kindness, to keep his Negroes healthy and contented. It was an obligation rarely shirked.

The Lower South before 1850 presented the anomaly of a society democratic in tone and professing democratic ideals, yet resting upon a highly aristocratic social and economic system. This appearance of contradiction was steadily rectified from about 1830 until 1860, when it finally disappeared. For the system to which the Lower Southerners owed their prestige and power speedily brought with it a new social attitude, a new philosophy, and a spade was called a spade, Democracy, except in stump speeches, went by the boards.

The Lower Southerners believed that leaders would arise from the caste system which they set about establishing. The great landowners were to be the rulers—as they already were—and there was to be an intermediate class from which the professional men, the lawyers and physicians, were to be drawn. These were to be educated at the public expense.

In 1846 Daniel Goodlow argued that Southern land would be worth as much without the Negroes, that capital which could be better invested otherwise was tied up in Negroes. But, the planters replied, the argument granted, what would become of the Negroes? Who would control and care for them? The problem was insoluble.

Yet the great wealth of the planter was illusory. Very little of his money stayed in his own pocket. The bulk of the profits from a cotton crop went to enrich the Yankee merchants who supplied the plantation with the manufactured articles necessary for its upkeep. The South was a source of enormous profit to the North, and the South resented her plight. The North, getting so much, began, under a panoply of moral purpose, to wonder why she didn't get more. Why not get it all? And so the air thickened as time went on.

Southern money stayed North, and Southerners clamored for a cessation of "paying toll to New England." Farsighted Southerners looked forward to building mills of their own, and the new plans were being discussed by the leaders. By 1860 cotton mills were running in South Carolina, North Carolina, Georgia, and Virginia.

The planter class, enjoying a perfect leisure under the slavery regime, devoted their energies to politics—which meant, after 1830, imperialistic expansion. The Mexican War had added New Mexico and California and extended the Texas boundary to the Rio Grande.

They dreamed of a great empire that would embrace, eventually, all of Latin America. The history of Congress after 1840, until 1860, is one of bitter struggle of the Southern politicans to gain the preponderance of power which would enable them to direct the politics of the country in the interest of their imperialistic dream. When Abraham Lincoln was elected on a platform of no quarter to the slavery expansionists, the planters prepared to leave the Union—but not primarily to realize their imperialism. They withdrew to perpetuate a stable and deeply rooted way of living, which, they foresaw, the restless industrial society of the North would gradually exterminate.

By 1860 the Lower South was a distinct nation. It differed from the North as deeply as the United States differs from Great Britain today. The war, for the Union, was justified by a fiction—that the states were one nation. When historians are far enough from the event, they will speak of the years 1861 to 1865 as the period of the dual Presidency. Their vision cleared, they will see the Lower South in its unique quality and wonder what, if it had been left alone, it might have become.

3 Davis and the Lower South

On a spring day of 1843 Joseph Emory Davis could be seen strolling in the extensive grounds of his great plantation, The Hurricane, in southwestern Mississippi. At his side walks a beautiful and clever girl, Miss Varina Howell of Natchez, whose father is his old and close friend. Miss Varina affectionately calls him Uncle Joe; she is seventeen—a young lady with her hair up—and she is paying Uncle Joe the visit he has been looking forward to for several years.

As they approach the house Joe Davis explains that storms blew parts of it down years ago, and that is why he calls it Hurricane. They enter a wide hall, open—it being warm in the early Southern spring—at both ends. The two rooms on the right are the drawing room and the tea room for the ladies; on the left are the bedroom of the master and the office. The lower room is the dining room, paved with red brick highly polished. Upstairs is the music room; the ceiling is arched, and the room is flooded with light. Here the children play charades or give mock concerts, and the guests play and sing. Around the walls hang the family portraits in heavy frame.

Joe Davis leads Miss Varina to a painting of a vigorous man of about sixty, handsome but gaunt; there is a certain distinction in the face, as there is in all portraits of this period, for the wandering artists who record the generation know best how not to offend their patrons.

After a moment, Davis says, "My father. He was a good soldier, a good citizen, a good master to his Negroes, and the best rider in the country—looked like one of Charles' Cavaliers on horseback—Jefferson reminds me of him at times so much that it startles me. . ."

The transformation of the Davis family in one generation from insecure small farmers into great planters typifies the rise of the Lower South. Typical of the Lower South, too, was the growth of the patriarchal idea, whereby Samuel Davis, a plain man, became the symbol of knightly grace—and the fountainhead of wisdom to his children.

The Davis family was in most respects typical of the population of the Lower South. They were, even in the generation of the distinguished Jefferson, a "new family," and they had in their veins none of the blood of the leading houses of the older parts of the South. But they were not the less typical for this or for their having originated in the North.

Jefferson's grandfather, Evan Davis, had been born in Philadelphia of Welsh immigrant parents in 1702 and had migrated to Georgia. By the time the American Revolution began, Evan Davis was dead; but his son, Samuel Davis, fought in many different commands in a fierce guerrilla war, for Georgia and the Carolinas were ravaged by wandering bands of the British and the Tories, or American Loyalists. He became captain of an irregular company, and at the end of the war was given land near Augusta, Georgia, for his military services and made clerk of the new county of Washington, then on the frontier. In about 1783 he was married to Miss Jane Cook of South Carolina, whom he had met during the war. Tradition makes her a niece of General Nathanael Greene.

It is certain that Samuel Davis was a man of fine character—well-fitted to sire the leader of a great society, all the great leaders of which came from much the same stock. After less than a decade of farming near Augusta, he left Georgia for the Kentucky wilderness. He settled in what is now Todd County, a little to the west of the extreme south central part of the new state, near the Tennessee line. He arrived in 1792; the first settlement had been made in that region only seven years before. He built a rude pioneer cabin. The farm was about 600 acres; the crops were tobacco—

the money-making staple—corn, and wheat. Samuel Davis raised horses, and he is supposed to have kept a tavern called Wayfarer's Rest, where he served food and drink to man and beast. He evidently liked his farm, for he stayed in Kentucky nineteen years. It was there that most of his children were born.

The tenth and last child of Samuel and Jane Davis was Jefferson, born on the Kentucky frontier farm on June 3, 1808. He was named Jefferson for the current President—the only Davis child who was not named from the Bible. Nothing whatever is known of his few years in Kentucky except that he was called Little Jeff, for, when he was three, the family moved again.

This time Samuel Davis decided to go south to the new cotton country, which was drawing thousands of men from the worn-out lands of the older South.

The residence in Louisiana was very brief. But the next homestead, in Wilkinson County, Mississippi Territory, was to be the last that Samuel Davis would build. His children needed a more settled life, and he was getting old; he was fifty-six in 1812. He at last became a good farmer—not rich enough to be called a planter—but now that his older children began to marry, all he could give to them, at each marriage, was one Negro slave. And that was all they ever got from him.

After 1812 lower Mississippi became a seething chaos of immigrants, whose violence was typical of frontier times. The old communities, founded under the Spanish regime, were broken up, and it was not till about 1835 that the interests of King Cotton became fixed and all parties admitted his rule. There were two principal towns—Natchez, the cotton market on the river, and Washington, where cultivated people of the old order lived. Both towns were scenes of political violence between the new, unwashed Democrats and the older, more respectable Federalists, or Whigs, as they now called themselves. Jefferson Davis, as a small child, went to the nearest log schoolhouse, where the teacher knew only the three R's. He picked cotton with his father and the Negroes in the field.

He had the usual amusements of boys in a primitive region. He hunted and fished; he had dogs, and he rode horses. He learned a great deal about the care of horses and their breeds, but he failed to master the details of the cotton industry, that unifier of Southern life, the one element in the Lower South that was definitely to distinguish it from other sections. When he was still a schoolboy, he came home one day saying that his teacher had assigned to him a lesson beyond his power to learn in the given time. His father promptly put him in the cotton fields, saying that he must choose labor or education. After two days of cotton picking, he chose the latter—not so much because it promised immunity to hard physical work, but, in his own phrase, because of the "implied equality" with the field hands. His father had evidently not objected to such an inference, and it was a disquieting tendency in the son.

In 1815, Jefferson then being seven years old, his

father sent him back to Kentucky to a better school. The school of St. Thomas Aquinas had been founded by four Dominicans in 1807, at Springfield, and here for two years Jefferson Davis studied his Latin grammar and lived in the room of one of the priests, Father Angier, because he was the smallest boy in school. At that time the best schools in Kentucky were run by Catholics. The Protestant clergy was not so well educated as the priests.

In 1817 Jefferson's mother insisted that he come home, which he did, and he was sent to schools nearer home until 1821 and his fourteenth year, when he once more started north to enter the freshman class of Transylvania University in Lexington, Kentucky. Again, but not for the last time, he was to come under influences different from those of the Lower South, for the atmosphere of Transylvania was then perhaps the most truly national of all colleges in America.

It was also probably the best college at that time and certainly the most popular. It had the largest student body in America when Davis enrolled and the best faculty; the courses were as advanced as at Yale or Harvard; the medical library was the best in the United States. The academic course was mainly the classics, with ancient history, mathematics, oratory thrown in. Davis became well-grounded in the classics, especially Latin, and formed the habit of omnivorous reading, so that he became the best informed, possibly the best educated, man in the United States Senate.

During his three years at Transylvania, Jefferson

Davis received the important groundwork of his education. Then his father, a few months before he died in the summer of 1824, got him an appointment to West Point. The appointment was dated March 11, 1824, and it was signed by John C. Calhoun, Secretary of War under President James Monroe. For the first time, but not for the last, the names of Davis and Calhoun came together.

Joseph Emory Davis, recently returned from Kentucky to Mississippi, where in Warren County he was starting his plantation, Hurricane, was now, as eldest brother, the guardian of young Jefferson. He urged him to accept the appointment to West Point, for he was too young to take a college degree and to begin life in the rough country of southern Mississippi. To this Jefferson agreed, but it was understood that after a year at the military academy, he was to go to the University of Virginia. However, he stayed at West Point, and a military cast of mind was to become habitual. His closest friends at the Point all became soldiers— Albert Sidney Johnston, with whom he is supposed to have fought over a girl; Robert E. Lee, who was noted at the academy for his humorless rectitude; Leonidas Polk, later famous in the Confederacy as the "fighting bishop." Davis was "distinguished in the corps for his manly bearing, his high-toned and lofty character. His figure was very soldierlike and rather robust; his springy step resembling the tread of an Indian brave on the warpath."

Nevertheless, he was among the first set of young men court-martialed for drinking at Benny Haven's, a tavern two miles from the academy grounds. He was charged with drinking "spirituous liquors," and his answer to the charge, even at this early date, was that of a strict constructionist. He said that drinking at Benny Haven's was nowhere *officially* prohibited in the regulations and that malt liquors were not spirituous. Davis was a very high-spirited boy, and life at the Point was monotonous in those days.

At West Point, Davis received his lowest marks in mathematics, his highest in rhetoric and moral philosophy. The main part of his education was as a soldier; mathematics he neglected for the theory of government and for wide but scattered browsing in history. But his general standing was not high; when he was graduated in the summer of 1828, as second lieutenant in the United States Army, he stood number twenty-three in a class of thirty-four.

In the minor accomplishments of war, Davis became highly proficient. He was military in bearing, and he preferred soldiering to any other career. He left West Point with an immense faith in "West Pointism"—the belief that only trained soldiers could succeed in war. He was, in fact, a martinet, and he was destined, in a great crisis, to relp upon his military education and to fritter away his energy signing commissions for second lieutenants. He took away from West Point two things: a belief in education as the remedy for all ills and a haughty pride, an impatience with the imperfections of simple men that would not be chastened out of him until years later, when, under guard, he paid a visit to Fortress Monroe in Virginia.

Lieutenant Davis now began his career as a soldier on the Northwest frontier, still farther than West Point from his own people. The new exile lasted longer than any of the others—seven years.

It was full of hardship, peril, and adventure. More than once he barely escaped with his life. The duty, nearly the whole duty, of the Army posts in the frontier country of Wisconsin and Iowa was to keep the Indians in check so that the settlers could get a foothold. Once Davis and a few men were chased by a band of Indians; both parties were in canoes, but Davis improvised a sail and got away. He was quick-witted, resourceful, and absolutely fearless. In a terrible winter he almost died of pneumonia, for, although he was sturdily built, his chronic nervous instability made illness go hard with him. But he was a good soldier in a kind of warfare that was hardly war; there were no large bodies of troops, and there were no complex problems of strategy. Davis' whole early career was to strengthen the illusion that he had great talent for war.

When Black Hawk was captured in 1832, Colonel Zachary Taylor appointed Davis as the chief's escort to Jefferson Barracks. Black Hawk respected the young lieutenant for his kind and courteous treatment, and Davis admired Black Hawk, who, he said, with characteristic unpolitical candor, was the real hero of the war. Davis was a promising young officer, but of another young man who served in the Black Hawk War, there is a different story to tell. Abraham Lincoln was a poor soldier, but when a great crisis came, he realized that he knew nothing of war and that he had everything to learn.

Taylor's appointment of Davis to command the guard of Black Hawk seems to disprove the belief that "Old Rough and Ready" had an instinctive prejudice against the somewhat fastidious young officer. Further disproof of that belief is that fact that Taylor knew that Davis was in love with his daughter. Taylor opposed Davis' suit for two reasons: the proud young man was penniless, and he would not be able to retire from the Army. The hard-bitten old Indian fighter may not have liked the young man's high-and-mighty ways, but the real objection seems to have been that he was a soldier. Taylor was dead set against letting his daughters repeat the hardships his wife had gone through. The young couple were equally set upon marrying, and after about four years of intrigue and hostility between father and would-be son-in-law, which almost came to a duel, Jefferson Davis and Sarah Knox Taylor were married at the home of her aunt, near Louisville, Kentucky, on June 17, 1835.

If Colonel Taylor's objection to the match was simply a dislike of having his daughter marry into the Army, Davis had already met it by resigning. His brother, Joseph Emory Davis, now rich, had met the objection to his poverty by giving him a plantation in Warren County, Mississippi, next to The Hurricane, and by selling Jefferson, on credit, fourteen slaves.

Jefferson Davis' life up to 1835 had been a miracle of good fortune, but he had learned almost nothing, for he had suffered no checks to his easy career. The son of a Southern pioneer farmer of less than moderate means, he had received the best education of his time, without any effort whatever on his part and without any of that enlightening adversity which alone seems to season the characters of men. His eldest brother, twenty-four years his senior, had immediately replaced his father and smoothed his path to the end. His intelligence and integrity had enabled him to take advantage of opportunities created for him by others; he had made none of these opportunities for himself. He was now about to set up as a cotton planter, on land won by the patient effort of another and not even inherited in the regular line of responsibility from father to son. It is no wonder that he never quite understood how practical affairs are carried on. He had not gained any discipline over his feelings, for this comes through adversity or through long training in a traditional ideal. Nor did he understand that moral and political convictions are the complex product of feeling, for he supposed these to be matters of reason. Before he entered politics, he was convinced that people who disagreed with him were insincere.

About seven weeks after the young couple had arrived at Brierfield, the new plantation, Mrs. Davis wrote a letter to her mother: ". . . Write to me, my

51

dear mother, as often as you can find time, and tell me all concerning you. Do not make yourself uneasy about me, the country is quite healthy."

But, .eager to get the plantation going, they stayed too long in Mississippi and got to Louisiana, out of the fever region, too late. At the home of Davis' sister, Mrs. Luther Smith, they both came down with malarial fever. Davis was too ill to be told how ill his wife was, but in her delirium she sang fragments of an old song, "Fairy Bells," and he came to her bedside to see her die unconscious. She had always said that she expected to die young. After a long struggle, Davis got well.

He returned to Mississippi, and the most important period of his life began. The shock of his bride's sudden death threw him in upon himself. He went little into the neighborhood society, and he became a studious recluse. How far this life was deliberate, it is difficult to say, but he was ambitious, and his brother was possibly even more ambitious for him. It was a time of preparation for politics. But it was a singular kind of preparation and better suited to a career of letters or of pedagogy. The theory of the state may be learned in the cloister but politics only in the street. However, Davis read enormously in history and the theory of government, and a political career was the only use such training could be put to.

His elder brother was in this period of seclusion from 1835 to 1845 almost his sole companion, and "the brothers occupied their evenings with conversations on grave subjects, and during the day found abundant occupation attending to their plantations." The grave subjects centered on the interpretation of the Constitution, which the wrangling over the tariff after 1816 and the ordinance of nullification passed by South Carolina in 1832 had made the leading issue of the South. Joseph Davis had a good library, and Jefferson was collecting one.

The democracy of the Davis brothers was a mixture of early influence and political insight. Samuel Davis, the poor farmer, was inevitably a Jeffersonian Democrat, while the rich, North and South, were Federalists, poor and Demorcatic, but the "rich and the well- or Whigs. The great mass of the Southern people were born"—Alexander Hamilton's phrase—were everywhere Whigs. The interests of the cotton capitalists were not, this early, differentiated from the interests of capital in general. But this differentiation of interest was coming, and Jefferson Davis, following Calhoun, foresaw it. It was to create the Southern Rights Party, which the Democrats absorbed, along with most of the Whigs. In the party unheaval of 1844 the Democrats became the conservatives of the South; Jefferson and Jackson were repudiated. When the cotton magnates went over to the Democracy, they joined hands with the poorer people, and in the end created a united South. It was this that Calhoun had worked for all along, and Davis was shrewd enough to see the necessity for it in advance of most Southerners.

As a planter, Jefferson Davis prospered, and yet he was constantly advised by his more experienced brother, so that it is hard to say what he might have done alone. He was more than kind to his Negroes; the Davis brothers introduced into the slave system certain reforms that were so successful that, after 1865, their Negroes were singled out as examples of the talent of their race for citizenship. It was forgotten that they had acquired their talent as slaves.

There was no corporal punishment given to the Negroes by a white overseer, for the overseer was a Negro; every Negro was tried for offense by a jury of his peers, who were not obligated by the master to return a conviction of whipping, although they sometimes did. Occasionally the master, who reserved the right of pardon, had to temper the severity of the Negro jury. Jefferson Davis and his overseer—James Pemberton, a Negro—were devoted friends. When the overseer came to see Jefferson Davis in his office, the master pulled up a chair and said, "Sit down, James." When James left, Davis gave him a cigar. James was always James, not Jim, as he would have been on most plantations; nor would Jefferson Davis permit the other Negroes to receive nicknames. "It is disrespect to give a nickname," he said. Every Negro who could make money for himself was encouraged. He did business with his Negroes, and at the end of one transaction he owned a Negro $2,000.

On a high bluff on the east bank of the Mississippi, near Natchez, stood an old-fashioned house called The Briers, very large and surrounded by verandas, the home of W. B. Howell, a wealthy cotton planter. Howell was a native of New Jersey who had come to Mississippi in about 1818 and married a Miss Kempe. The Kempes were Virginians; Mrs. Howell's father had migrated to Mississippi early enough to fight under Andrew Jackson. The family of The Briers were thus typical of the Lower South, where all sections of the country were represented. The old town of Natchez, composed of three streets running one way and four the other, had gone ahead of Washington, the old social capital; it was now, in 1843, the center of the Whig, the planter aristocracy of that region. In the midst of Third and Fourth Streets stood the white-columned courthouse. Swaybacked old gentlemen slowly walked through the courthouse yard; young men, dressed in bright blue or light brown coats with silver buttons, cantered by on fine horses; great family coaches, preceded by black outriders, the gilded family arms glistening in the semitropical sun, clattered and bumped on the hard clay streets.

A year ago Joseph Emory Davis had asked his old friend, Howell, to let Miss Varina come to visit him at The Hurricane, but the answer had been that Miss Varina, then sixteen, might not come until the next year, when she had finished her course in the classics. She was a remarkably clever girl, and she was receiving an unusual education for her time, under the guidance of old Judge Winchester, a scholar and jurist from Salem, Massachusetts. The classics seem to have been covered by December, 1843, for, after the usual domestic flutter with silks and needles, Miss Varina, chaperoned by her tutor, set forth on the palatial steamboat *Magnolia,* on the journey to the Davis family.

Late in December Miss Varina Howell arrived at Diamond Place, the plantation of Mrs. David Mc-Caleb, a sister of the Davis brothers, fourteen miles north of The Hurricane, near Vicksburg.

At seventeen, Miss Varina was a fully developed woman, well-educated and trained in the responsibilities of her station in life. Her family had been quickly absorbed into the Southern scene, although they kept some of their Yankee traits; the daughters were taught how to cook and do housework—knowledge that was not likely to endear Miss Varina to the ladies of Virginia should she ever be brought among them. She was very handsome and very healthy; her dark hair, dark eyes, and dark skin glowed with youthful vitality, and her full upper lip gave to a haughty bearing a slight expression of cruelty, a trait which she did not have.

After she had been at Mrs. McCaleb's plantation only a few days, a handsome and handsomely mounted horseman rode up and, dismounting, gave her a message. He was, he said, on his way to a political meeting in Vicksburg.

A few days later Miss Varina wrote to her mother:

Today Uncle Joe sent, by his younger brother (did you know he had one?), an urgent invitation to me to go at once to "The Hurricane." I do not know whether this Mr. Jefferson Davis is young or old. He looks both at times; but I believe he is old, for from what I hear he is only two years younger than you are. [He was thirty-six.] He impresses me as a remarkable kind of man, but of uncertain temper, and has a way of taking for granted that everybody agrees with him when he expresses an opinion, which offends me; yet he is most agreeable and has a particularly sweet voice and a winning manner of asserting himself. The fact is, he is the kind of person I should expect to rescue me from a mad dog at any risk, but to insist upon a stoical indifference to the fright afterward. I do not think I shall ever like him as I do his brother Joe. Would you believe it, he is refined and cultivated, and yet he is a Democrat!

She called these words her first impressions, but they remain the most penetrating analysis that the character of Jefferson Davis ever received. She was, indeed, a remarkable girl, but it is doubtful that she had ever again the detachment to look at him so coldly; she was to see him again and again.

The evening passed. The brothers discussed, but so complete was their agreement that they seldom argued their politics. Poems were recited, and there were readings from historians. When the brothers were tired, when Jefferson's eyes felt strained, Miss Varina read to the company, and she translated with perfect accuracy the Latin quotations in the texts.

Every day Miss Varina, being a staunch Whig, wore

her subtreasury brooch. This Whig emblem was a small cameo upon which was carved a watchdog, a bloodhound crouching by a great strongbox, heavily locked.

One day Miss Varina appeared without her brooch, and Jefferson Davis knew that he had won; it was her way of telling him that she had put aside her family prejudices. These were strong but not insurmountable, for Howell, upon whose consent the engagement depended, was, as one writer calls him, the "complete father," and the question of party was waived, because Jefferson Davis was a cultivated and a very promising man. The lady had been quickly won, for Davis left The Hurricane in January—a few weeks after Miss Varina had arrived—an engaged man. It was 1844. On February 26 of the next year they were married, and the Whig ladies of Natchez shook their heads. The bride's trousseau was simple and the ceremony almost plain—a concession to a simple, plain, and Democratic man.

The young couple went to live at Brierfield. It was a simple, rambling, one-story frame house, with a small portico in front and still smaller porticos detached on the two wings. The Jefferson Davises were good planters, but they were not typical planters; for, even before their marriage, Jefferson Davis had actively entered politics, and they were not, from now on, to be much at home again.

In 1843 he had run for the state legislature in his district, which was overwhelmingly Whig; he knew that he had no chance to win, but the Whigs defeated him only by withdrawing one candidate and concentrating their vote upon the other. The successful candidate was Seargent S. Prentiss, the most famous orator in the South before the rise of William Lowndes Yancey. Against him, Davis held his own and attracted attention. The next year, 1844, while he was courting Miss Howell, he "stumped" the whole state as an elector for James K. Polk. In 1845 he was elected to Congress as representative at large.

His career in Congress was cut short by the Mexican War. Davis resigned his seat in the House and raised a volunteer regiment, later famous as the Mississippi Rifles. Colonel Davis was a strict disciplinarian, and he had advanced ideas about war. He armed his men with a new model of rifle, which he preferred to the old musket which the War Department clung to. His men became the crack volunteer organization of Zachary Taylor's army, which they joined in September, 1846. There was fighting at Monterey in which Davis took part, and he did more than any other of Taylor's subordinates to win the Battle of Buena Vista. The Mexican cavalry charged up a ravine on the flank of the Mississippi Rifles, but Davis threw his men around the end of the ravine and poured a converging fire upon the Mexicans that broke the charge. The battle was won. Colonel Davis, wounded in the foot, went home on crutches, the hero of the hour. The mob cheered him in New Orleans, and he was eulogized by the great Prentiss. He had always thought of himself as a soldier; in a sense he had reached the zenith of his career. He seems to have believed the applause.

Whether he was a great soldier, no one can decide, but the popular belief that he was became one of the instruments of his fate. He had received an education that he had not earned; he had set up as a planter through another man's labor; now, without great political experience, he was sent to the United States Senate in 1847, in recognition of his military prowess. His career now resembled the economy of people who lived by taking in one another's washing. His war record advanced him in politics and his political record, in 1861, justified his election to the Southern Presidency when the need of military talent seemed urgent. Not even the devils in hell, who have much knowledge of frailty, could have withstood the vain conclusion that so rapid and so unearned a rise to leadership was due to personal merit so great that men could not fail to recognize it. It is probable that Davis secretly took this view, for when people disagreed with him, he felt personally insulted. A man who had served a full polical apprenticeship could never have fallen into such an error. But the studious, neurotic egoist, poring over his books, had that pride of intellect that feeds on seclusion. He could not manage men, and he was too great a charter to let men manage him; that was the tragedy of his career.

Davis was occasionally duped. He had been in the Senate only a year when he became the most eloquent defender of Southern rights—the obvious successor to

Calhoun. When the Compromise of 1850, framed by Henry Clay, had been ratified by popular vote in Mississippi, he did not hesitate to resign from the Senate to run for Governor on the anti-Compromise ticket —an act of self-sacrifice that, for a time, seemed to end his political career, for he was defeated. But Pierce called him to the Cabinet, as Secretary of War, in 1852. In 1854 the Kansas-Nebraska issue of squatter sovereignty held the political stage, and Douglas duped Davis into its support. Davis thus helped to bring on the South the disastrous experiment of trying to hold its own in the territories; the failure of this effort may be said to be the direct cause of the Civil War.

As Secretary of War, Jefferson Davis dominated a mediocre administration and told Pierce to do everything but say his prayers. He enlarged the United States Army; he pushed on the work of completing the Capitol. But all the time he was using his power in the Cabinet for other and more far-reaching ends. His greatest aim was Southern expansion into Mexico and Cuba and Central America.

Only the extremists, like Yancey and Rhett, knew that the South could expand no farther, but Davis, after 1850, was definitely on the side of maintaining the rights of the South inside the Union. When the Wilmot Proviso, prohibiting slavery in the territory snatched from Mexico, had been put aside by the Compromise of 1850, he took heart; and he was optimistic after the Dred Scott Decision, in which Chief Justice Roger Brooke Taney laid down that the Missouri Compromise had been unconstitutional and that slaves could be held in territories North and South. The South was now apparently at the height of its power, but the power was weak, because it lay in the letter of the law, which the North would no longer stand by. Davis, the constitutional pedant, could not see this, and he never understood the political reality behind the political law. Every breakdown of political theory gave him a shock, and this was mostly what he received from the election of a sectional President, Abraham Lincoln, on November 6, 1860. He no longer had the capacity to learn.

After his farewell to the Senate, Davis lingered vainly in Washington, in the hope that the threats of his arrest would be carried out and the right of secession tested by law. He then started for Jackson, Mississippi, making speeches on the way in southwestern Virginia, northern Georgia, and Tennessee. At Jackson, he remained a week, where, as head of the Army of Mississippi, he set about procuring guns, clothing, ammunition.

When Davis left Jackson for Brierfield, he had the position that he coveted above all others—the highest military rank in the state, the position for which he thought himself best fitted. In this contented frame of mind he had spent a few days at Brierfield "repairing his fences," when a messenger arrived with a telegram from Montgomery, which informed him that he had been unanimously elected President of the provisional government of the Confederacy.

4 The Making of a Nation

DAVIS' inaugural speech was unremarkable except for one thing; it foreshadowed the passive, defensive policy that the Davis government maintained throughout the war. Reaffirming the legal and constitutional right of the South to withdraw peacefully from the Union, Davis argued, with a certain show of plausibility, that the North could have no economic interest in bringing the South back and that the interest of Europe lay in preserving peace so that cotton could flow undisturbed into the European mills. In the midst of the unreality of the inaugural address he inserted a plea for a large army, to be put immediately upon a war footing. He did see that war was coming, but beyond this he did not know what to do. He was worried.

The first problem that confronted him was the creation of an Administration, and in this he exhibited some of the limitations of a conventional and routine mind. The choice of his Cabinet was the product of political habit. Instead of getting the best men available, he followed the custom of apportioning out the offices evenly among the states, and in order to bind them together, he carried the procedure farther than it had ever been carried before. There was no party boldly grabbing the spoils; every state, he supposed, had to get its share, and it got it. Davis' political blindness was never darker than in the formation of his Cabinet. He seems honestly to have thought that he was conciliating all parties with his even division of the honors. What he actually did was to eliminate from his government the powerful radicals and to antagonize them. He evidently did not foresee this, for all of his well-meant efforts were incredibly naive.

Since South Carolina had led the secession movement, it appeared unrgent to give that troublesome state all the honor it was due. For this reason alone, the portfolio of state would not have been too great a reward, and Davis accordingly offered it to Robert Barnwell, who turned down the offer. However, he asked for the Secretaryship of the Treasury, not for himself, but for Christopher G. Memminger, an unimaginative little man, who, by industry and conservatism, had risen from a Charleston orphanage to local prominence. What Davis failed to see was that neither Barnwell nor Memminger belonged to the Rhett faction; they were both moderates. Memminger was generally unknown and disliked where he was known.

Toombs was again disappointed, for next to the Presidency, he desired the Treasury, and it was the position above all others that he was best fitted for. In a region where economists were few. Toombs was an economist and a good one, and he would have seen that the finances of the Confederacy were not those of a local bank; he would have taken chances. Since both he and Georgia had to have something, he was juggled into the State Department. Toombs' ability was so various that he would have made a good Secretary of State had Davis let him alone. But Davis was master of his Cabinet, and the belief of Toombs and Rhett that they would control the foreign policy quickly went up in smoke.

There was Yancey, who, along with Alabama, deserved his share; but he was a difficult problem. He was a lawyer, an orator, and an agitator, not an administrator. So he was offered the post of Attorney General, the least important in the Cabinet. He promptly rejected it. But Yancey, like Barnwell, had his man. He proposed Leroy Pope Walker for Secretary of War. Davis, a trained soldier himself, knew that war should be administered by a man who has better qualifications than a heart in the right place; he had in mind Braxton Bragg for the job, but so great was his desire to please, so anxious was he not to hurt anybody's feelings, that he discarded Bragg and gave the place to Walker. The result was that Davis became Secretary of War himself—probably his intention all along. Three days after his inauguration he began writing detailed instruction about caps and friction primers and rifling machines to purchasing agents, adding that the contracts would be signed by the Secretary of War! It is no wonder that the Cabinet complained that they were mere office boys. Davis was qualified to give advice in war, but the only department that was not interfered with was the Treasury, the one that needed interference most.

There was one department that did not object to interference; that was the department occupied by Judah P. Benjamin. First, Benjamin had been Attorney General—the post which had turned out to be Louisiana's share and which Benjamin, willing to bide his time, had alone been willing to accept. When Walker gave up the War Department for lack of occupation, Benjamin was promoted. He was not a bad Secretary of War, but the military reverses during his regime discredited him, and his scalp was demanded. Davis acceded to the popular will by again promoting him, this time to Secretary of State! Benjamin's talent was diplomacy, but in 1862 the chances of Confederate success in that field depended upon miracles. Benjamin soon learned that the plain speaking of Yancey and Toombs and Rhett offended a President who would brook no open opposition, and he tempered the wind to the sensitivity of the shorn lamb and became, as all flatterers become, indispensable. He is prominent in Confederate history because he symbolizes the President's weaker self.

The one Cabinet appointment that was unequivocally good was that of Stephen R. Mallory of Florida to the Navy Department. The success of the appointment was accidental; Mallory had been chairman of the Navy Committee in the United States Senate, and he was appointed because Florida had had to have "something." The appointment, besides, was honorary; Davis at first did not plan to have a Navy. But when the Federal blockade made one necessary, Mallory gathered about him the best talent in the land. The Confederate Navy, created out of nothing, was the marvel of the world. It demonstrated for the first time the power of ironclad vessels; it used the first underwater torpedo; it launched the first even partially successful submarine.

One other Cabinet appointment was good. John H. Reagan of Texas, whose state early in March became the seventh in the Confederacy, was Postmaster General; he did all there was to do with a difficult but unimportant office. Mallory and Reagan were the only original appointments to keep their offices throughout the war.

When Mrs. Davis and the children had arrived in Montgomery, the Davis family went to live in a plain, two-story frame house, where Mrs. Davis, whose skill at political management exceeded her husband's, received visitors and occasionally held a reception. Davis was already too overworked to unbend to the politicians, but when he was not harried by care, he could be charming; at any rate, he often laughed at the blusterers who shouted that the Yankees would not fight.

He rose early, working at home until breakfast, went to his office, returned to work again, frequently until midnight. The Confederate offices were in a large, boxlike, ugly, red-brick building situated on a corner. No attempt had been made to give it the outward signs of majesty and power. The inside walls were white-washed. Important offices were designated with hand-written sheets of paper pasted on doors. The President's office, upstairs, stood in the center of a quadrangular gallery, and the sheet of paper on his door simply said THE PRESIDENT. There was always a mountain of papers on his desk, but he was accessible to everybody. Officials came in without a word; strangers required the intercession of an usher; no one was refused an audience. Democracy reigned supreme.

Congress had wasted time making speeches, and though Davis showed a strong will, his hand was weak because he knew not what to do. The most urgent problem of the new nation was its relation to other countries, including the United States. The stand of the Federal Government would be decided largely by the attitude of the European powers, for Europe's recognition of the Confederacy would put it immediately upon its feet. From the outset, President Davis knew this; until 1864, when he was finally convinced that "we have no friends abroad," he depended upon European recognition for the solution of his difficulties. How, in the light of his own estimate of Europe, as this was revealed in the instructions to his emissaries, he could have expected aid from abroad, is one of those mysteries of human character that we shall never see through.

Yancey, as we have seen, had not yet been disposed of by the government, so he was selected to head a commission to Europe. He was not fitted by nature or training for the task; he was impetuous and proud, and his experience was that of a provincial statesman. Bargaining sense and humility and patience before rebuff were necessary to the success of the mission, and because Benjamin had these diplomatic assets, he would have been the best man for the place. There was talent in the Confederacy, but it was never properly used.

Just after Yancey had received his instructions— March 16, 1861—he went to see Rhett, with whom he agreed on the necessity of commercial treaties. But he surprised Rhett by saying that his instructions gave him no power to make them. "Then," said Rhett, "if you will take my advice, as your friend, do not accept the appointment. For if you have nothing to propose and nothing to treat about, you must necessarily fail. Demand of the President the powers essential to your mission or stay at home."

The instructions had been written by Toombs, as Secretary of State, at the President's direction, in a colorless lucidity that seems like irony. The letter was long, very full—of nothing. In the end it said two things which were different ways of saying that Cotton was King. The North, Toombs said, would, in case of war, be cut off from the profit on manufactured goods sold to the South and from the exchange of the South's raw materials; therefore, "we have no unusual reasons to fear war." And then, Cotton being King, all that was necessary to bring Europe to the South's feet was a "delicate allusion to the probability" that the cotton supply would be cut off.

It has been said that Rhett shared this delusion, but it is doubtful. The delusion took no account of the fact that in 1861 England had so much raw cotton on hand that even in 1862 considerable quantities were sold back to American mills. When the Commission of Yancey, Rost, and Mann went abroad, hostilities had not begun; how Davis hoped to coerce Europe with a situation that had not yet come about, it is hard to see. Commercial treaties alone would have succeeded. When Yancey had returned early in 1862, he said to Rhett, "You were right, sir, I went on a fool's errand."

Possibly it was sheer economic ignorance that prompted Davis to such a futile policy, or possibly he really believed that Europe would be impressed morally by the Southern case against the usurpations of the North. All of Davis' thought ran on a plane considerably higher than the reality of human conduct, and it is certain that he would have been moved by a vindication of abstract principle anywhere. He was very much the saint in politics. While the fire-eaters were motivated by a single and powerful desire to be rid of the United States at any price and were thus not so much vindicating an idea as asserting a desire, Davis was always the American standing for the principle of local self-government. He would not sell out to Europe; he would not let Europe get a stranglehold on any part of *America*, for the South was undoubtedly still America to him. Rhett's distrust of Davis, from Rhett's viewpoint, was justified. Davis' early training had kept him from being molded into a typical Lower Southerner, and although he fiercely insisted that the separation of the states was eternal, this was mostly the position of stubborn pride. Mrs. Davis testifies that up to the fall of Sumter, his whole thought—certainly his unconscious thought—was bent upon reconciliation and reunion. It is a curious fact that the Americanism of the opposing White Houses was equally intense, though of different kinds.

The finances of the Confederacy were based upon the Kingship of Cotton, but the government evidently expected the monarch to act from sheer nobleness; he was never offered a bribe. Stephens urged the immediate export of 2,000,000 bales of cotton to establish a secured credit abroad of about $500,000,000; it was a good idea, but the 2,000,000 bales were not available (many had already been shipped), and there were no ships to carry them in. Such, at least, was the plausible argument of Memminger. There was a large fleet of steamers that the South might have bought, but they were dismantled, and there was no way to fit them out.

Still, the possibilities of getting sound money were not exhausted. The remaining cotton of 1860 and the whole crop of 1861 could have been bought up as collateral for a foreign loan and shipped in small lots or held till after the war. This would have saddled the Confederacy with a huge debt, and Memminger, straining at the gnat of bold economy, later swallowed the camel of timid bankruptcy and defeat. He let the cotton alone and issued an unsecured currency, which at first bought gold at par; but because its value depended upon the quicksand of public opinion as to the Confederate morale at different times, it was worth no more in 1864 than the paper it was printed on. Money backed by cotton would have been superior to currency dependent circumstance. Memminger's way of coercing Europe to intervene by putting His Majesty, Cotton, on a pedestal, instead of degrading him to the marketplace, was, undoubtedly, the easiest way. However, it assumed that the unbought cotton, for an indefinite period (Davis predicted a long war), would virtuously stay where it was put.

Three things happened to the cotton. It was sold by Southerners to Union merchants; often this was done under pressure of starvation, but oftener by profiteers, who soon made up a new class of "cotton snobs." Or it was confiscated by the Union armies where they overran the cotton belt. Or it was destroyed by Confederate garrisons retreating before the superior numbers of the enemy. To protect cotton that was eventually to be lost without having done the government any good, large detached bodies of troops were scattered around the South, and the main armies were weakened.

Nevertheless, the feeble foreign policy and the short-sighted economy cannot be charged to Davis as positive blunders; a few men rose above those errors, but not all; there were prevailing superstitions, and Davis was only one of their victims. But they were far-reaching. In spite of the mistakes of leaders, of the dissension among the people, of the lack of grand strategy in the field, the Confederacy came within a hairbreadth of success; its entire history is a mosaic of tremendous *if*s. *If* any one set of unfavorable circumstances had been warded off, the South would doubtless have won. The failure to secure real money and to bribe the good offices of Europe set the Confederacy, at the outset, all awry; it was a bad start from which it never recovered.

Early in March Davis' masterful personality had triumphed over the Lower Southern politicians. Affairs everywhere were in the hands of those who not only hoped, but believed that "peaceful councils would prevail."

Two weeks went by. Lincoln had been inaugurated, and Seward, the new Secretary of State, refused official reception to the Southern emissaries. However, through John A. Campbell of Alabama, a justice of the Supreme Court and a last-minute Unionist, he had unofficial intercourse with the Confederates, and he constantly promised that Fort Sumter would be evacuated. There is reason to believe that Seward's representations were sincere; he probably had peace ideas of his own, which he held in contempt of what he thought was the weak policy of Lincoln, and he pre-sumed to give promises that Lincoln knew nothing of. But Lincoln, a masterly politician, was playing for time, waiting for an opportunity to put the seceded states popularly in the wrong. The opportunity quickly came.

While the Confederates were being deceived by Seward, Lincoln was preparing—after some hesitation—to send an expedition to Charleston to reinforce Major Robert Anderson in Fort Sumter. The preparations were secret; the attitude of the Federal Government toward South Carolina and the Confederate Government was an ingenous tissue of lies. If there initial lies saved the Union, the moral, for those who like a moral, is that the end justified the means. Lincoln was now in a position to make Fort Sumter a test case. Would the Confederates tamely give up to the Federal Government property in a Southern port that they claimed as their own—or would they seize the property by force and thus give Lincoln the chance to say that the Southerners had shed the first blood?

This was too easy, and the Confederates were to blame for their delay. Other property had been seized; other shots fired. If Fort Sumter had been seized earlier, Lincoln would have been compelled to look farther than the firing on the United States flag as an excuse to invade the Southern states. His sole excuse would have been the questionable legal obligation to bring the states back into the Union, and in this he would have gained scant support in the North; the attitude there was unwarlike and in favor of "letting the erring sisters go." Could he, somehow, get the Southerners to fire on the American flag? If so, he would have a popular, emotional appeal to make to the Northern people.

The Confederacy was in a tight spot. It had no desire to make war, and, even if it had, the time had passed to begin it; Lincoln had been established and had got the situation in hand. The anxiety of the Confederate Government to prove that it had no aggressive intentions had counseled delay, and delay was about to precipitate it into what would seem to be aggression in the eyes of the world.

On April 6 Lincoln signed the order for the expedition to Fort Sumter. In Montgomery, Toombs advised the Cabinet to delay; the time for a bold step, in his opinion, had passed. The only thing to be gained by taking Sumter was a technical vindication of states' rights—a slight point beside the advantage of waiting till Lincoln was forced into the first overt act. President Davis sent to General Pierre Beauregard, commanding at Charleston, through the Secretary of War, the following order:

If you have no doubt as to the authorized character of the agent who communicated to you the intention of the Washington Government to supply Fort Sumter by force, you will at once demand its evacuation, and, if this is refused, proceed in such manner as you may determine to reduce it.

This was all, but it permitted Lincoln to put the responsibility of starting the war upon the South.

On April 11 Beauregard demanded the surrender. Anderson refused but said to the messengers that he would have to surrender on the fifteenth or starve. So Beauregard wisely did nothing that day. At midnight a harbor pilot brought news that a Federal vessel was standing off the harbor. Beauregard knew that the Federal relief squadron had come. After one o'clock he sent a new demand to Anderson, for the circumstances that would have forced the surrender would, within twenty-four hours, be removed. Anderson refused a second time. The aides, without reporting to Beauregard, left Sumter for Fort Johnson, where they gave the order to fire.

At dawn of April 13 General Anderson began firing back, but the walls of Sumter were crumbling; the Federal fleet outside the bar could not come to its relief; early in the afternoon Anderson raised the white flag. Anderson and Beauregard exchanged high courtesies, and the surrendered garrison, after saluting the Stars and Stripes, marched out with colors flying. Not a man had been killed in battle on either side.

The Southern public thought it was a great victory, and Charleston was delirious for days. But it was a political triumph for the North; Europe had no interest in the actual merit of the Southern case, and Sumter enabled Seward to tell England that the South had brought on the war. The day after the fall of Sumter the war party in the North clamored for action; where there had been one man in ten willing to coerce the seceded states, there were thousands, certainly a majority, eager to "defend the flag." Few Northern men understood the masterly game that Lincoln had played, for when Lincoln, on April 17, called for 75,000 three-months men to deal with "combinations too powerful" to be suppressed by the action of the courts, they rose as one man. It was all in vain that Davis pointed out the absurdity of the idea of "combinations," by means of which Lincoln made the Southern situation out as one of rebellion; it was too late to expect a populace to understand that the "combinations" were a whole people, that the courts themselves were a part of them, that the South had not rebelled against any authority that it recognized. Lincoln declared a blockade of every Southern port, from Virginia to Texas, but the South scorned it; it could not, of course, be made good.

Davis called for 100,000 men to serve for one year. He had a clearer view of the magnitude of the coming struggle than Lincoln had, but this view contained contradictions. He saw that the war would last longer than three months, but he took no vigorous steps to arm the men. By the end of 1861 Confederate purchasing agents were more active than their Federal rivals, but in the early months Davis seems to have depended on seizing old arms scattered around in state or federal arsenals. There were about 150,000, only 10,000 of which were modern weapons. There was little artillery and no machinery to make it; the few cannons on hand were old, many of them left over from the War of 1812.

By taking the first step at Sumter, the Confederate Government had to prepare for war under great disadvantages—that is, after hostilities began. Thus, the initiative was lost. Toombs had favored delay, and now he urged aggressive action, but there was no way to take it. Davis' defensive attitude was due partly to lack of equipment, partly to his conception of the war. He hoped to gain moral prestige in Europe by the integrity of his defensive position, for already—astonishingly enough—he looked to Europe to end the war. It would have been better to do nothing before Sumter than after, for that display of fireworks gave Lincoln an immediate war aim that the populace could understand.

There was a great uprising in the South, too. More than 300,000 men answered the call to arms. The Southerner, bred to horseback riding and the use of firearms, was the finest military material in the world, incomparably better than the town-reared clerks and mechanics of the North. But the Davis government was not in a position to use the enthusiasm of the Southern masses; not all of the 100,000 called for were accepted; there were no materials of war.

On April 17, the day Lincoln called for 75,000 men, Virginia at last seceded, and the peace convention crashed against the stone wall that it had not been able to see. In a few weeks the second group of states— North Carolina, Arkansas, and Tennessee—following

Virginia's stand against coercion of the cotton states, left the Union. The hesitation of Virginia had lost for the Confederacy the crucial border states of Maryland, Kentucky, possibly Missouri. Lincoln threatened to arrest the Maryland legislature if it voted secession; he convinced the Kentuckians that the war was not against slavery, but for the Union, and they were won; through the energy and skill of Francis P. Blair, Jr., he was able to hold Missouri. If Virginia had acted sooner, Lincoln might not have had time to deal with the other border states. Maryland in the Confederacy would have meant the loss of Washington, D.C., to the North; Kentucky would probably have brought Missouri with it and possibly southern Ilinois and the lower counties of southern Indiana.

The loss of these states did not directly defeat the Confederacy. But the circumstance was decisive; with them the Confederacy would have won. Lincoln knew this. He said, "I think to lose Kentucky is very nearly to lose all." So he wheedled and coaxed. The Southern politicians, using the King Cotton logic, threatened; they expected economic determinism to bring Kentucky and the West to their side, but they failed to see that the West had acquired interest in the East that it had lacked in 1850.

Virginia at once sent a delegation to Montgomery to make a treaty with the Confederacy, and its head, Robert M. T. Hunter, became, until the fall of 1864, one of Davis' staunchest friends. How much Hunter had to do with one of the chief mistakes of the Southern politicians is not know, but it was speedily made at this time.

The wives of the politicians were dissatisfied with the village atmosphere of Montgomery, and the politicians themselves, used to the comforts of their trade, chafed at the restraints of the two hotels and the numerous homes that had taken them in. Congress resolved to hold its next session in Richmond. The President protested, but upon the invitation of Virginia, it was decided to move the whole government there. Virginia was no longer as powerful as any one of the great Lower Southern states, but she was still the "Mother of States and Statesmen," and her prestige was tremendous. Besides, she had almost failed to secede, and, like Georgia, deserved the utmost consideration of the Confederate Government.

Davis' protests were in vain. The removal of the capital to Richmond placed it on the frontier, where it required the maximum of military protection, without any strategic advantage whatever. The strategic center of the Confederacy was the Mississippi Valley, and the capital should have remained there. For political reasons, a large army was kept in Virginia; another in the West for strategic purposes. Thus, the military power being divided, there was never a unified strategy on a grand scale. The East and the West fought separate wars. The somewhat factitious value of the Richmond capital blinded the government to the enormous and actual value of the Mississippi Valley.

Davis set out for Richmond late in May. His popularity was still high, and he was greeted everywhere on the way with overwhelming enthusiasm. He was still riding the wave of war emotion. In Virginia he was received with the honor due a second George Washington.

Davis was now at his best. At this early period, before the responsibilities of the war had borne heavily upon him, he was a star able to shine in the most brilliant society, and he shone. But the Virginians had their reservations. Who was Jefferson Davis? They had never heard of his grandfather, nor did they know the number of his slaves. The prejudice against Davis was, however, less personal than section. The Virginians were a self-sufficient people, provincial to their very eyes, backward-looking and contented to rest upon a mellow classicism that had followed the era of the great Virginia statesmen. They had no sympathy with the Lower Southern dream of a great empire, and there is no doubt that they looked upon the Lower Southerners as upstarts.

After about six weeks the Davises moved into the former residence of Dr. John Brockenbrough, a mansion at the end of East Clay Street, looking over the brow of a tall hill. The citizens wished to give them the house; Davis insisted upon paying his rent.

Every day the President rode out to the training camps north of the city. Sometimes a numerous staff accompanied him, but more often his sole aide was his private secretary, Burton Harrison, a Louisianian of Virginian descent, whose perfect linen and perfect manners survived all the shocks of war. "Mr. Davis rode a beautiful gray horse," Harrison said. "His worst enemy will allow that he is a consummate rider, graceful and easy in the saddle."

Troops were being rushed to Virginia from all parts of the South, and now the President had given over the finances to Memminger and had disposed of foreign affairs. He devoted his energies, which were enormous, to the organization of the Army. The largest until accepted was the regiment, to the disgust of the governors of states, who, for political reasons, wished to appoint their own brigadiers. Davis reserved the right to appoint the officers of higher rank, and because there was a great wealth of trained soldiery in the South, the Confederate Army at the start was better commanded than the Federal, whose officers at first were mainly politicians. Yet the Confederate Army, in view of the immense enthusiasm, was absurdly small. Davis would not accept organizations for short terms of services; at a glance this policy seems farsighted, but the reason why he stood by it was undoubtedly the lack of any large plan for the conduct of the war. His policy was to stand indefinitely on the defensive, to be indefinitely ready for any move on the part of the North.

Beyond the rapid concentration of an army in Virginia, there was no positive military plan. A bold and enterprising leader—not merely a cautiously tenacious one—would have rushed the purchase of arms in the early months and pushed an army of 100,000 men against Washington by July, or advanced into the Northwest and cut the North in two. But Lincoln was gathering a force for the defense of Washington, and Davis, without a positive strategy of his own, took the negative step of placing his forces where they would meet the Federal invaders whenever they chose to move. On a larger scale, this became the Confederate strategy for the war.

At this time the governors of the states supported the Confederate Government, and most of the state troops were mustered into the Confederate Army. Officers who had resigned from the United States Army were given corresponding ranks in the Confederacy, and when the Congress provided for five full generals, Joseph E. Johnston of Virginia should have headed the list. Instead, the five generals were ranked as follows: Samuel Cooper, a New Yorker who had married a Virginian, was given, for some reason, the highest rank as adjutant general, but he was a harmless mediocrity; Albert Sidney Johnston, an able soldier and a truly noble man; Robert E. Lee, who had been offered the command of the Union forces but was not much talked of otherwise; Joseph E. Johnston; Pierre Beauregard, a fair soldier and the most distinguished rhetorician of the Confederate Army.

Joe Johnston attributed his failure to get the highest rank to Davis' personal dislike, which did not exist, and he never forgave it. Nor was the President the man to deal lightly with a subordinate who questioned the motives of his authority. The quarrel, which was to outlast the Confederacy, had a paralyzing influence upon its career.

By the second week in July, the Confederates had three small armies in the Virginian field. Their positions were strictly defensive. The largest force, under General Beauregard, occupied Fairfax County, to oppose a Union force under Irvin McDowell, which was rapidly approaching 50,000 men; Beauregard had about 20,000. The Confederate flag, flying from Munson's Hill, was in plain view of Lincoln in the White House. The towns of Alexandria and Arlington Heights, opposite Washington, were not occupied by Federal troops until late in May. The Confederates might have taken both places, and from Arlington bombarded Washington, but these important steps were not taken. In the Shenandoah Valley, Joseph E. Johnston had about 9,000 effective troops against 14,000 Federals under General Robert Patterson. The Confederates were outnumbered, but they held the interior line. By means of the Manassas Gap Railroad, Johnston and Beauregard could reinforce each other and concentrate enough men at either threatened point to offset the originally superior numbers at that point. Another small force, about 2,000 men, under General John Magruder, guarded Old Point Comfort—the approach to Richmond by way of Fortress Monroe up the James River. The feverish activity of the Union Army under McDowell and the cry of the Northern press of "On to Richmond!" made it plain that there would be a battle soon.

On July 13, 1861, Beauregard came to Richmond, where he met Davis, Cooper, and Lee in Davis' parlor; it was the first Confederate council of war. Beauregard wanted to attack McDowell before he advanced farther in Virginia with his own and with Johnston's command. McDowell's army was poorly organized, and the Confederate troops, man for man, were at this early period far superior to the Union troops, so the plan might have succeeded. But it involved risks, and these Davis was not willing to take. It was safer to let McDowell make the first move.

He was not long in making it. By July 18 his advance guard had reached Bull Run, some thirty miles from Washington, D.C., and on that day fought a slight engagement with the Confederates, who held the south bank of the creek. Davis telegraphed Johnston to move his army to Beauregard's assistance. By the night of the twentieth, about 7,000 of Johnston's men had arrived; one of the brigades was commanded by an obscure and eccentric officer named Thomas J. Jackson. The opposing armies were now about equal —though the Federals had better artillery—for McDowell had been able to bring only 30,000 men to the field.

Next morning, July 21, he surprised and crushed Beauregard's left flank, and early in the afternoon the roads to the rear of the Southern army were packed with stragglers and demoralized fugitives. President

Davis had intended to get there before the battle began —perhaps, since he still thought of himself as a soldier, to step on the field and lead his men to victory. But the Congress had convened on July 20. Beauregard may have foreseen the President's wish, for he sent him no warning, and Davis was delayed.

When his train arrived in midafternoon at Manassas Junction, the signs of defeat were so obvious (to the civilian eye) that the conductor would not let the train go farther. But the engine was detached, and the President and his party reached the field. He made addresses in fine style to the fainthearted troops, and he was cheered. He came upon a dingy officer who was holding out his hand to a surgeon to have a wound bandaged. "Give me ten thousand men," the officer was saying, "and I'll be in Washington tomorrow." The President inquired what troops were these standing about doing nothing, and urged them to join the fight. Jackson, the wounded officer, coldly replied that the troops were his and that the battle was won. The last Federal troops were disappearing over the Stone Bridge in the direction of Washington. Davis went on, promising the famished men that rations would be sent to them, and such was his influence upon the battle.

Jackson's brigade, standing "like a stone wall" in a pine thicket, had saved the left wing from destruction, and the arrival of Kirby Smith's brigade had turned defeat to victory. Both sides had fought well, but both were undisciplined, and the luckier side won. Lest the advantage be lost, Davis called a war council and urged Johnston and Beauregard to the pursuit. But neither of these generals nor Davis himself knew the extent of the victory. They offered excuses—there was no transportation; there were not enough supplies; the men were disorganized; there were the forts of Washington. Ten thousand men could have marched to Washington unopposed and ended the war. Maryland would probably have seceded, and the Lincoln government could not have survived the blow.

The Battle of Bull Run, or First Manassas, had been, in itself, insignificant; only 18,000 men had fought on each side. But it is not too much to say that the first battle was decisive of the war. Never again did the Confederates have such a chance to take Washington. The inactivity which followed the battle gave the North time to raise a great army: Lincoln asked Congress for 400,000 men and $400,000,000, and the organization of the Union Army, under General George B. McClellan, proceeded methodically all summer, without the slightest interference from the Confederates.

Davis was not satisfied with the failure of Johnston and Beauregard to pursue the enemy after Manassas, but he had no other generals who had proved more enterprising, and he could arrive at no positive plan of his own. The Southern volunteer, reflecting opinion at home, believed that the war was over, that the Yankee would not fight, and by the close of the summer, Johnston's army at Manassas—Beauregard had yielded the command — was so reduced as to be inefficient. The fire-eaters were everywhere disaffected, for Davis was doing nothing while the gigantic preparations of the North went steadily on.

There was no real fighting in the East for the rest of the year. Davis, not being a man of action, had no strategic plans, but he gave an almost fiendish energy to the details of war. From the very beginning he administered the Army as if he were Secretary of War in Pierce's Cabinet in a time of peace. There was no bold originality of organization. He divided a beleaguered nation into military departments, each with a head responsible to him alone. There could be no cooperation on a grand scale.

The inactivity of the government had permitted the popular overconfidence to undermine the war spirit. At the beginning of the new year, McClellan's army totalled more than 100,000 men; another Federal army of about 30,000 threatened the Shenandoah Valley. Johnston, at Manassas, had fewer than 40,000, and Jackson, to meet 30,000, had only 4,000 men. In the West, Albert Sidney Johnston had been able to raise only about 30,000 against an army of 100,000, which General Henry W. Halleck was preparing for the capture of the Mississippi Valley.

The North, at the beginning of 1862, had a sound military policy. East and West, the utmost pressure was to be put upon the Confederacy. While the South, after Manassas, settled into the secure sense of being a nation which was on the verge of winning its independence, the North gained time, which was practically all it needed—a commodity that the South could not afford to lose. The stage was set for the direst calamity, but the way Davis met it was to be the surprise and admiration of the world.

5 The Great Year: 1862

BY THE MIDDLE of February, 1862, disasters had fallen upon the Confederacy, from one of which, at least, it never recovered.

In about the middle of January, General Ambrose E. Burnside sailed with an expedition from New York to the Carolina coast, where, after more resistance from rough seas than from a Confederate army, he easily captured Roanoke Island and got a foothold for the invasion of the South by way of the sea. This, in itself, was a slight victory; it would be quickly neutralized if the main Confederate armies could defeat the large Union armies opposed to them.

By February 1, General Albert Sidney Johnston had about 40,000 men for the protection of Tennessee. A large detachment of this force, under Polk, held Columbus, Kentucky, on the Mississippi; on the extreme right, at Bowling Green, Kentucky, Johnston himself watched the menacing attitude of a Federal army, larger than his own combined, under General Don Carlos Buell. A small force garrisoned Fort Henry on the Tennessee River, and a larger army, about 15,000, held Fort Donelson, on the Cumberland. If the Federals could take these two forts, the other Confederate forces would have to fall back into Mississippi or Alabama, and the Federal armies, by using their powerful fleet of transports and gunboats, could move unopposed into the heart of Tennessee.

At this point Ulysses C. Grant, who years before had retired from the regular army "under a cloud" of drunkenness and had difficulty getting even a subordinate command at the beginning of the war, now for the first time came upon a scene that he was later to dominate. At the beginning of February he started from Cairo, Illinois, with 15,000 men and 4 ironclads under Flag Officer Foote, and steamed up the Tennessee River. On the sixth, he telegraphed Halleck: "Fort Henry is ours. I shall take and destroy Fort Donelson, on the eighth." But Grant was delayed; he did not reach Fort Donelson, twelve miles away, until the twelfth. On the fifteenth the Confederates, who slightly outnumbered the Federals, tried to cut their way out, and would have succeeded had not Generals Gideon Pillow and John Floyd suddenly become demoralized; they withdrew to the fortifications. That night Pillow and Floyd escaped, leaving General Simon Bolivar Buckner in command, and Colonel Nathan Bedford Forrest got away with his cavalry. Next day

Grant received reinforcements bringing his army to 27,000 men. The case was hopeless. On the sixteenth Buckner surrendered 12,000 men, 20,000 rifles, 48 cannons, 17 heavier guns, about 3,000 horses and an immense quantity of supplies. Beauregard had urged Johnston to concentrate his army at Donelson and to take command in person. But Johnston, the great hope of the South, had shown little enterprise; he should doubtless have ignored Buell, heavily reinforced Fort Donelson, and crushed Grant.

The fall of Donelson and the capture of Roanoke Island came to the South as a slap in the face from an old and trusted friend. The situation was inexplicably reversed; in the summer the enemy had been turned back from the gates, but now the South, before it knew what had happened, had lost Kentucky and Tennessee and was thrown on a perilous defensive. The public, of course, cried for a scapegoat, and Johnston, an idol a few days before, was bitterly attacked. A deputation from Tennessee went to Richmond to demand his removal, but Davis firmly replied, "If Sidney Johnston is not a general, I have none to give you." Davis' support of Johnston is one of the most attractive incidents in his career, and the exchange of letters between the two men exhibits human nature at its rare best. Johnston made no excuses, saying that "the test of merit in my profession is success," and he refused to answer the public howl. Davis' confidence in him remained unshaken. The confidence was well-placed, and yet its proud contempt of public opinion was a little disquieting, and it was later to bring nothing less than havoc on the cause of the South.

One scapegoat was not enough; Davis himself was the real point of attack, and the politicians cannily singled out the hated Benjamin as the President's most vulnerable spot. Walker had resigned in the summer of 1861. If Toombs, in the State Department, had been a clerk, Walker had been, in the War Department, a mere office boy. Benjamin, having made himself useful by never contradicting the President, had been promoted to Secretary of War. His scalp was demanded as an atonement for the disasters to the Southern arms. Instead of gratefully delivering Benjamin up and thus conciliating the opposition, Davis promptly let it be known that Benjamin was not at fault. As if ironically, he removed Benjamin from the War Department and made him Secretary of State. The opposition was infuriated. Benjamin's promotion was a far-reaching mistake; it sealed the opposition in their hatred of him, and now, for the first time, there was a powerful, outspoken anti-Davis party.

On February 19, three days after Donelson, Davis wrote privately to General Joseph F. Johnston at Manassas: "Events have cast on our arms and hopes the gloomiest shadows, and at such a time we must show redoubled energy and resolution." Is it possible that Davis felt that he had not acted with enough resolution? The story of the chances of European intervention will detain us elsewhere; it is certain that Davis had depended upon them too much, that their failure had caught him without alternative measures. In this harrowing crisis, the permanent government of the Confederacy was installed on Washington's Birthday— the day Lincoln had ordered an advance of all the Federal armies—and even the weather conspired with the despair men felt of what the future was to bring.

April came, and so did new disasters, but still the South was without a great army to roll back the Federal tide. After the fall of Donelson, Albert Sidney Johnston collected his scattered forces at Corinth, Mississippi, about twenty miles south of the Tennessee line. He was still the object of bitter attack, so he offered the command to Beauregard, who had been sent to serve as his second in command. But Beauregard refused it. By April 1, Johnston had about 40,000 men, ill-armed and badly supplied. Braxton Bragg's corps from Pensacola had joined, but there were other considerable forces which, because of the departmental system, were not at Johnston's disposal. Grant, commanding the right wing of the Union Army, was concentrating at Pittsburg Landing on the Tennessee River, twenty-five miles from Corinth. He had somewhat fewer than 40,000, but Buell was rapidly approaching with nearly 40,000 more.

Johnston decided to attack Grant before Buell arrived. The attack was scheduled for April 5, but the inefficiency of the corps commanders delayed the march, and it was not made until dawn of the next day. However, the attack was a surprise—Grant was not even on the field—and until an hour before nightfall, it swept everything before it. The Union Army was on the very point of annihilation, but Johnston had been killed, and Beauregard, with an hour of daylight left to complete the victory, ordered the attack to cease. Two miles behind the front line, he did not know that Grant's army was a horde of demoralized fugitives huddling on the bank of the river. That night Buell's army arrived, and next day the Confederates were driven from the field. This battle, named Shiloh, from a log church where Beauregard had his headquarters on the second day, was the greatest struggle that had taken place in America up to that time. The South lost more than 10,000 men and the North 13,000. One day's delay had turned certain victory into defeat.

Now Johnston, abused before the battle, was praised to the skies, on the theory that if he had not been killed, the battle would have been won—which is possibly true. Yet Johnston had nowhere fulfilled public expectations. And Beauregard became more and more unpopular, till finally Davis removed him from the command, on the pretext that he had deserted his army. Beauregard, a fine soldier whose one great weakness was overcaution, was too ill to remain in the field. His successor was Braxton Bragg, a good organizer, like General McClellan, and like McClellan again, utterly incompetent in the face of impending battle. His appointment was one of the few great mistakes that Davis made in selecting his generals; indeed, it may be said that it was his only mistake, for all the others, as we shall see, came out of the complications caused by this single one.

The Confederate hope was to sink still lower. While Shiloh was being fought, Island No. 10, in the Mississippi, the only strong fortress on the river north of Vicksburg, surrendered to the Federals with about 7,000 men. At the end of April, New Orleans, the largest and most important city in the South, fell under the attack of Admiral David Farragut's gunboats and was occupied a few days later by an army under General Benjamin Butler. Butler's treatment of the inhabitants was brutal in the extreme.

By May 1 the Confederate line in the West had been pushed back 200 miles, from Columbus and Bowling Green in Kentucky to Tupelo, Mississippi. The upper and the lower Mississippi were in the hands of the enemy; only Vicksburg and the batteries at Port Hudson, Louisiana, maintained connection between the East and the rich country—rich in men and supplies —west of the river. In Virginia the whole northern neck, the country between Washington and the Rappahannock River, was in Federal hands. McClellan had transferred his great army to Fortress Monroe to attack Richmond from the southeast; he outnumbered Joseph E. Johnston more than two to one. The passive and dispersive strategy of the South had brought her to the brink of ruin.

By the end of February, 1862, Jefferson Davis saw that European intervention—chief resource of victory up to that time—would not come soon enough to win the spring campaign. He changed his policy. It is by no means easy for a man to unsettle all his confirmed habits of thought and to strike out vigorously in a new direction, but Davis did this. And the new policy marks him as a great man.

The greatest need was a large army, which alone would rescue the Confederacy from its imminent peril, and Davis knew there was only one way to get it—conscription. After weeks of discussion in Congress, a bill was passed on April 16, providing for the drafting of all citizens between eighteen and thirty-five. The twelve-months men, whose discharge was almost due, were retained in the service automatically for three years from the date of their original enlistment. It was to retain these men, whose release would have meant the collapse of the Southern Army, and also to stimulate volunteering, that the draft bill had been passed. Thousands of men joined the Army to escape the odium of conscription, and by midsummer of 1862 it numbered in the field about 400,000 men.

By the middle of June the great armies were gathered that enabled Lee and Jackson to win the victories of the Seven Days Battles, Cedar Mountain, and Second Manassas.

It was Davis who gathered them, and to his courage and determination in the crisis, credit is due. There had never been a draft in American history, and the very idea was repellent to Americans, particularly in the individualistic South. But there was no other way to save the country, and Davis, knowing well the storm of opposition that would meet the draft, willingly undertook the responsibility.

By the late spring Jefferson Davis was at the height of his power. He had thrown every minor consideration aside in order to create a great army, and for this he had flouted, in temporary necessity, the principle that the South stood for. He knew the risk he took. "If we succeed," he said, "we shall hear nothing of these malcontents; if we do not, then I shall be held accountable by the majority of friends, as well as foes." His eyes were open, and only a great and fearless character would have plunged into those extreme measures that might have saved the South.

Now occurred one of those events that people have been wont to ascribe to fate or to the irresistible merit of Lee. To Davis alone the honor is due for the recognition of the genius of Lee.

After the Battle of Shiloh, there was, for some months, almost no fighting in the West, but by April, in the East, the stage was being set for that moving drama of arms that gave the Army of Northern Virginia an imperishable fame in the annals of war. By May 1, Joseph Johnston had moved his whole army of 53,000 men to the peninsula between the York and James rivers, where he opposed General McClellan, who had about 105,000 men. The Confederates won a small rearguard action at Williamsburg, but McClellan was slowly pushing them back, until at last Johnston, whose weakness was unwillingness to face the issue of battle, had retreated almost to the suburbs of Richmond. The President, riding out to the camps, suddenly came upon a park of artillery on the edge of the city. Having refused to interfere with an officer in the field, he had not known that Johnston had retreated so far. Johnston had not kept him informed. Davis demanded a battle—which Johnston at last delivered on May 31. The retreat had been highly strategic, for it ended with the Union Army being divided by the swampy and difficult Chickahominy River, and Johnston attacked the isolated corps south of the river. If the subordinate officers had been equal to their jobs, the Battle of Seven Pines would have been a great Southern victory. It ended a drawn battle, but the advantage remained with the Confederates. Johnston, an able soldier, but not the man for the crisis, was wounded. Davis, without the slightest hesitation in the face of hostile opinion, appointed Lee to the command. Seven Pines checked McClellan, who was morbidly cautious, and gave the Confederates what, at the moment, they most needed—a great leader and more time.

While Lee was strengthening the defenses of Richmond, Jackson in the Shenandoah Valley was fighting a small, brilliant, and highly important campaign. With a force never larger than 18,000 men, he routed armies totalling more than 60,000 and threw the North into panic lest he should take Washington. Lincoln, who at this time had not learned the danger of controlling armies from an executive's desk, played his forces into Jackson's hands, sending detachments needed by McClellan to capture Jackson, who defeated and eluded them all. McClellan being thus crippled— though his single army outnumbered all the Confederates in Virginia—Lee swiftly transferred Jackson to Richmond, where the united forces reached about 90,000 men, the largest Confederate army ever in the field.

Now that Stonewall Jackson had dispersed McClellan's reinforcements, Lee moved swiftly to the execution of his plan to raise the siege of Richmond. The entrenchments were easily manned by less than a third of Lee's army, and the remaining 60,000 men were liberated for a most audacious offensive. Lee, following Napoleon's rule, had not failed to study the character of his opponents; he knew that McCellan was overcautious and vacillating and that he supposed the Confederates numbered at least 200,000 men. When Lee divided his army, McClellan was firmly convinced that he had the 200,000; for, without that number, he in Lee's place, would never have undertaken so bold a plan. On June 26, 1862, Lee threw his army upon the 30,000 Federals that were isolated north of the Chickahominy River, under General Fitz-John Porter, a distinguished soldier. The Seven Days Battles had begun.

Not only anxiety, but a desire to lead armies and to participate in battles kept Jefferson Davis daily at the front. He still believed in his own military gifts.

At the engagement at Ellerson's Mill, which opened

the Seven Days, Davis appeared and found Lee busily giving orders to his staff. Shells were bursting nearby, bullets singing in the air. Lee nodded coldly to the President and, pointing at the President's numerous staff, asked with some asperity, "Who are all this army of people, and what are they doing here?"

Davis, startled by the brusque reception, replied, "It is not my army, General."

"It is certainly not my army, Mr. President," said Lee, "and this is no place for it."

"Well, General, if I withdraw, perhaps they will follow." Davis, in the embarrassed silence, rode away, but not from the field. He concealed himself behind an embankment, not from the enemy's bullets, but from the more terrifying Lee.

The day after Ellerson's Mill, the great battle of Gaines' Mill took place. Porter was overwhelmed, but he was not annihilated, as Lee had hoped he would be; he made good his retreat to the south bank of the Chickahominy, where he joined McClellan's main body. Lee expected McClellan to retreat down the peninsula, and he delayed a day for the retreat to begin. During this one day McClellan was retreating to the James River; Lee's miscalculation had saved the Army of the Potomac from destruction. McClellan could not fight, but his retreat was masterly; at Malvern Hill he turned and gave Lee a bloody check. Yet the retreat continued with the protection of the gunboats on the James, for McClellan was demoralized.

There, in an unfortified camp at Westover Landing, he might still have been destroyed if he had been pursued more closely. At a famous council of war held at the Poindexter mansion near Malvern Hill, Lee permitted the cautious President to overrule his desire for vigorous pursuit. Jackson alone sat in dour and impatient silence.

Lee's great victory changed the whole character of the war. The finest army of the Union had been put on its back for several months, and the initiative was in the hands of the Confederates. But, again, Davis' caution had its influence upon Lee. The President could not believe that McClellan was utterly disposed of, and a proposal from Jackson, made right after the Seven Days, went unnoticed—Jackson proposed to ignore McClellan and invade the North with 60,000 men. By the middle of August, when it was certain that McClellan, now reduced to a mere corps commander, had withdrawn from the peninsula, this was done. But by that time a reorganized Army of the Potomac, under General John Pope, who had captured Island No. 10, was organized and in the way.

Lee now moved to suppress Pope before McClellan's corps could reinforce him. Lee, still studying the character of his opponent—who this time was a rattle-brained braggart—contemptuously divided his army, sending Jackson with about 25,000 men to Pope's rear at Manassas Junction. Jackson cut Pope's communications with Washington and burned millions in supplies. Lee followed with the rest of his army at a distance of fifty miles. Jackson held Pope at bay and even deluded him into thinking that he had gained an advantage; then Lee arrived. Next day the united Confederate Army crushed and routed Pope, 55,000 against 70,000, and threatened Washington. This great battle, Second Manassas, was a strategic and tactical masterpiece, perfect in every detail, Napoleonic in its conception and performance. From this time Lee's prestige rose, never to sink again.

Nevertheless, Lee was in a dilemma; he had defeated Pope, but he was too weak to besiege Washington. What should be do? He wrote to the President that he could not afford to be idle but that he lacked equipment for an invasion; his army had few wagons, and his men were without shoes. Davis, for the moment, was directing most of his attention to the West, where Bragg promised success; but he gave his consent to Lee's invasion of Maryland, actually a more risky movement in 1862 than it would have been in 1861, when the Federals were ill-prepared to meet it. However, the rewards of success would be great, and Davis had unreserved confidence in Robert E. Lee.

The antiwar party of the North was clamoring for peace, saying that the mightiest of armies had not been able to defeat the South, and the belief in the invincibility of Lee had spread to England, where agitation for recognition of the Confederacy was redoubled both by James M. Mason, who had been sent there as the Confederate commissioner, and by his friends in Parliament. When Lee crossed the Potomac on September 2, 1862, more was at stake than even Davis realized; Mason had been told that England would await the results of the Maryland campaign. Men everywhere believed that now the South would win.

Lee moved into western Maryland, near Hagerstown, and by the middle of the month his army, ill-fed and barefoot, had lost heavily through straggling and numbered altogether not more than 40,000 men. In the crisis of the North, McClellan, though bitterly hated by the radical Abolitionists because he was a Democrat, was restored to command. Faced with the character he knew, Lee again divided his army in the menace of still greater odds, sending Jackson to capture Harper's Ferry, which fell, with a Union loss of 12,000 men. Lee, at this juncture, would have done well to return to Virginia; yet he knew that a victory over McClellan would mean Southern independence, and he was willing to run all risks. The Union army sent to pursue him numbered 87,000 men.

Lee had depended upon McClellan's vacillation for time to rest his army and to gather his stragglers, but McClellan came on swiftly and took him by surprise. One of Lee's generals had lost his copy of the order containing the Confederate plan of campaign; it was found in Frederick, Maryland, and taken to McClellan. Jackson rejoined Lee just in time for the bloody Battle of Sharpsburg, known in the North as the Battle of the Antietam, which in some respects was the greatest feat of Southern arms. Again, Lee had fought a perfect battle and, with 39,000 men, defeated every attack of 87,000. The Federals, recently defeated, moved without flinching to the charge; the Confederates, meeting them "with a steadiness more than Roman," hurled them back till at nightfall the ranks of entire Confederate brigades lay dead in the line. But Lee lacked the men for a counterstroke, and he was forced to retreat into Virginia.

Nothing but fame was won by the battle of Sharpsburg, for a tactical victory was turned, by retreat, into a strategic defeat which permitted Lincoln to issue his first Emancipation Proclamation and shook the belief that Lee could perform miracles. British intervention was consequently indefinitely postponed. Sharpsburg was as decisive a battle as Gettysburg, just as First Manassas was more decisive than either. The longer the war lasted, the smaller the chance the South had to win. But Lee's great campaign had convinced the North that the easy victory expected in the spring was not to be won. Richmond was out of danger, and would be for two years, while Washington was menaced again and again. A month after Sharpsburg, Lee's army rose to 78,000 men, not the largest, but the best and most seasoned that he ever commanded.

In the West the Confederate offensive led by Braxton Bragg was rolled back without a decisive battle. Davis had entertained great hopes of this invasion of Kentucky, but at the outset the campaign had two

106

handicaps that were insuperable. First, it was undertaken, as Joe Johnston querulously but truthfully said,
without fighting the opposing army. Not the Union
Army but the Kentucky country was the mistaken
objective of the campaign; Lee had defeated the army
opposed to him before he invaded Maryland, and
Bragg should have defeated Grant and Buell before
he marched north into Kentucky. He entered Kentucky with a powerful, undefeated army on his track.

The second handicap to the invasion was the faulty
character and the incompetence of Bragg himself; he
was capable of energy of the hysterical kind only, and
when that failed, he invariably found a scapegoat to
bear the blame. The rank and file did not trust him—
a bad sign—and his officers, William Hardee, Leonidas Polk, Nathan Forrest, and John Breckinridge had
lost all confidence whatever in him.

The failure of the Confederate offensive on three
fronts—Maryland, Kentucky, and Arkansas, where
Earl Van Dorn, with a small army, had been driven
back—was followed by great depression throughout
the South and by renewed bitterness from the anti-
Administration men. The pressure of the Federal
blockade was at last reducing the population to want,
and Mason, in England, could no longer pretend that
it was not effective. It was now almost impossible to
ship cotton in large quantities; the little that went out
of the country made huge profits for the speculators,
who hoarded their gold. Paper money was steadily de-
clining; its value depended not upon securities, but

upon military success. Lee had won great victories, but victory short of complete independence was defeat.

The months of July and August, 1862, were undoubtedly the peak of Davis' career, from his own viewpoint. He had raised, in spite of bitter opposition, a large and powerful army; he had supported on his own responsibility an officer who twice defeated an army larger than his own and fought a drawn battle north of the Potomac, threatening Washington. He had, in short, emerged from imminent defeat to the offensive, and victory appeared to be at hand. Although the Confederate offensive had momentarily failed and could not be attempted again with the same advantages, the outlook—except to a prophet, and prophets were rare—was brighter in November than it had been in May. But the public and the repudiated radical leader were dissatisfied with anything less than victory, and Davis does not appear to have estimated correctly the meaning of the failure of the Maryland campaign. He did not see the importance of offensive war to the cause of the South.

If the President was temperamentally and politically set against aggressive warfare, he was equally jealous of his territory, and if he could avoid it, would not give an inch. It was for this reason that he had divided the country into departments of scattered garrisons; he hated to yield country even temporarily until he was compelled to—and thus the Confederacy was "nibbled away." The small garrisons fell one by one till there was nothing left, and while the process was slower than it might have been if Davis had concentrated his armies, the result was the same, without possible success. This policy crippled the Confederacy in the last campaign of 1862, when Lee might have ended the war with one stroke.

After Sharpsburg, Lee fell back unmolested into Virginia, McClellan following very slowly and at a distance, and for the second time in six months, General James Ewell Brown "Jeb" Stuart, with his cavalry, rode around the whole Union Army. McClellan, prodded by Lincoln, crossed into Virginia with an excellent plan of campaign. It might have succeeded, but on November 7 he at last fell a victim to his own cautiousness and to his political enemies in Washington and was removed from the command. Ambrose E. Burnside succeeded him. This officer, thoroughly incompetent and so thoroughly honest that he admitted his incompetence not only to himself but to Lincoln, did not desire the position, but he obeyed orders. President Lincoln was so disappointed at the results of the summer that he urged Burnside to advance on Richmond, in spite of the approach of bad weather and the difficulties of Virginia mud. Burnside was not slow to advance. He decided to march to Richmond by way of Fredericksburg.

Lee and Jackson urged Davis to let Burnside cross the Rappahannock at Fredericksburg unopposed.

They wished to lead him away from his communications to the North Anna River and to compel him to fight with his back to the stream, where, if defeated, his army would be destroyed. But between the Rappahannock and the North Anna lay thirty miles of Virginia territory which Davis was not willing to give up without a fight; he preferred the ultimate risks of indecisive victory to the temporary loss of ground. He told Lee to oppose the enemy at Fredericksburg. There, also, Burnside had a river at his back, but beyond the river rose high hills from which artillery could protect an army, no matter how badly defeated. Lee himself was partly to blame. He was something of a governmental martinet, and he would not override the constituted authority of the President—an authority that had only as much permanence as he himself could give it by force of arms.

On December 13, 1862, Burnside hurled column after column against Lee's almost impregnable position; at nightfall about 13,000 Federals had been slaughtered; only 3,000 Confederates fell. The Union army was demoralized, an the most demoralized man in it was Burnside; he was beside himself, and wished to hurl more columns against Lee the next day, but his officers refused to lead them. At the end of the battle, Lee could not deliver a counterstroke under the powerful Federal batteries across the river. There is little doubt that Burnside would have been destroyed elsewhere. The Army of the Potomac was to have other bad commanders, but Burnside was heaven-sent, and Lee would never meet his like again. Jackson was enraged and desperate that Burnside should be so sorely beaten only to escape, and he asked Lee to launch a night attack, tying white rags to the sleeves of the Confederates to distinguish them from the enemy; the Federals were crowded on the riverbank, and the attack would have been highly successful butchery. Lee refused. It was not his idea of playing the game. Jackson played only one game—the game that wins.

The two armies went into winter quarters, and the fighting of 1862 came to an end.

6 Gettysburg and the Military Crisis

THE TROUBLE brewing in the West at the end of 1862 was remotely the fault of Davis himself—the fault of the dispersive departmental system under which a commander in one place might be hard pressed but powerless to call for aid from another officer standing idle fifty miles away. The Department of the West was larger and more important than that of northern Virginia and much farther from Richmond; what it needed was a general with independent power who could transfer troops without Davis' consent and practically conduct an independent campaign. Davis saw this necessity, but whether it was unwillingness to meet it in any case or the lack of a general whom he trusted that stayed his hand, it is hard to say. At this point, the influence of James A. Seddon, the new Secretary of War, was felt. Seddon, a shrewd Virginia lawyer, had no military experience, but he had military sense.

By the middle of November, 1862, Joseph E. Johnston, who had been wounded at Seven Pines some months before, said that he was ready for service, and Seddon persuaded Davis to send him to the West and to give him the control of the Army of Tennessee, under Bragg, and the Army of Mississippi, under General John Pemberton. These forces had so far acted without concert, and disaster in the West had seriously detracted from the importance of Lee's victories in the East. Johnston was one of the three or four best soldiers in the South; but he tended to avoid assuming responsibility; he was touchy and quarrelsome—other dyspeptic, and his instinctive dislike of offensive warfare had, inconsistently enough, undermined the President's confidence in him since his retreat up the peninsula before McClellan in the spring. In the end, Davis' lack of confidence may have been sheer dislike; Johnston had not handled him, in his rancorous letters, with kid gloves. So, when Johnston went West, his instructions were a little vague. They should have been full and explicit, for otherwise a general who hated responsibility would be cautious and timid, fearing that disaster would be charged to him if he exceeded the letter of his orders. Seddon had had Johnston appointed, but he could not get Davis to give him unlimited power. The result was that Johnston used less power than he really had, and the Confederacy, in the West, soon found itself between the devil of Johnston and the deep blue sea of Davis.

In the first week in December, Davis set out for the

West, arriving in Chattanooga on the ninth. There he had a conference with Johnston, the two chief subjects of which were Bragg's fitness for his command and the question of reinforcements for Pemberton's army, which was sorely threatened by an expedition of Grant, who was now beginning his operations against Vicksburg. Johnston supported Bragg, in spite of the wholesale disaffection of his officers and men— Cheatham said he would not serve under him—because he dreaded taking the command himself. But he urged that Pemberton's reinforcements be sent from Holmes' army of 30,000 men in Arkansas, which, under incompetent leadership, was soon to be frittered away. Holmes' department, magnificently called the Trans-Mississippi, was inviolable; and Davis, instead of sending Holmes an order, offered only a suggestion, which, of course, was not heeded. The President then went to Murfreesboro, Tennessee, to see Bragg's army and to decide whether the reinforcements could be sent from it.

He returned from Murfreesboro to Chattanooga and telegraphed to Seddon: "Found troops in good condition and fine spirits. Enemy is kept close to Nashville, and indicates only defensive purposes." The Federal General William S. Rosecrans indicated only defensive purposes until 10,000 men had been sent from Bagg to Pemberton, reducing Bragg to 33,000 to his own 40,000; then he swiftly took advantage of the situation to march with all speed upon Murfreesboro.

Meanwhile, Davis and Johnston went to Vicksburg to inspect the fortifications and to form a plan of action. No conclusion was arrived at. At Vicksburg there was a garrison of about 6,000 men and another of 6,000 at the only other Confederate stronghold on the river, Port Hudson. Pemberton's army had about 40,000; here were more than 50,000 men who, concentrated, would have made a larger army than the force that Grant was bringing against them. United with Holmes, Pemberton—if he had possessed the ability—could have taken the offensive against Grant. But Davis did not feel like interfering with Johnston; beyond the request for Holmes' army, Johnston did not wish to upset the status quo. He was contented to let two incompetent generals blunder away. After the initial error of weakening Bragg's army, Davis' responsibility for the disasters of the summer of 1863 in the West ceased; Johnston's began.

From Vicksburg the President went to Jackson, where he received a most enthusiastic welcome and made a great speech. He would have done well to make more speeches, to take more trips. He constantly forgot that the Confederacy was a political experiment and that the people were not fixed forces to be called into action by executive order; they needed to be coaxed and coddled, and he deprived them of the kind of public performance that they most loved —oratory from their leaders. In no sense was Davis ever the leader of the Southern people as a whole, and this was due to his complete lack of demagoguery, to his high opinion of the public intelligence. He sincerely expected the populace to understand the high motives of his close application to the details of office. But his infrequent public appearances had great effect, and more work of that kind and less attention to the claims of Captain Jones or of Lieutenant Smith for some obscure command would have done much to save the South. Disloyalty and despair, even at this early date, were rife in Tennessee and north Alabama, but instead of meeting this disaffection sympathetically, Davis could only issue proclamations holding it up to shame.

From Jackson he went to Mobile, where he was again cheered and praised. Then he returned to Richmond, discouraged and worn out.

While the President was still in Mobile, Rosecrans was continuing his march from Nashville to Murfreesboro to attack Bragg in his weakened condition. On December 31 the two armies clashed, both generals taking the offensive at the same time. But the Confederates, fighting with a valor and ferocity unsurpassed in the war, crushed the right wing of the Federals and gained the upper hand. Thereupon Bragg, demoralized as usual, settled down for a wait of two days, during which Rosecrans restored his lines. The second Confederate attack was repulsed. The Confederates, knowing well that they were ill-led, threw themselves headlong against the strong Union position and lost 10,000 men out of 33,000; the water in Stones River ran red with blood. A great victory had been thrown away; for Bragg had to retreat to Tullahoma to a weaker position, where it was difficult to keep the army supplied.

The Battle of Murfreesboro alone is enough to refute the belief that the Western Southern armies were inferior to those of the East; they were as well-organized—and for this Bragg deserves credit—and they were as well-equipped. On the whole, the quality of the men was better than in the East. The sturdy pioneer type had not disappeared in the West, and there were whole regiments of the "tall men," the six-footers from Mississippi and Tennessee. They fought as bravely and as devotedly as the men of Lee, and if they accomplished less, it was because they had no Lee at their head.

The dissatisfaction of the Army of Tennessee with Bragg's leadership reached its climax immediately after the Battle of Murfreesboro. He blamed his officers for his failure and threatened to court-martial General Polk, who, under the circumstances, had actually done his duty to the fullest. But the intense dislike of Bragg could not be ignored, even by Bragg himself, and he now did what no leader can ever afford to do and retain his prestige. He called his subordinates together—the subordinates whom he had recently blamed—and asked them to vote on his competence to command an army! Generals have always called councils of war and taken advice, but never before or since has an officer displayed such weakness of character. The proceedings alone, even without the subordinates' verdict, stamped him as unfit for his office. The subordinates voted that he had lost their confidence and the confidence of the army as a whole.

In the face of this, Davis could not sustain Bragg any longer. He had Seddon telegraph Johnston to relieve Bragg and to take command of his army in person. Seddon had been working all along for Bragg's removal, and his success witnesses the extent of his influence with the President. Bragg was Davis' close personal friend, and while he would permit someone else to remove him, he would not do it himself. He passed the responsibility on to Seddon and Johnston, and Seddon left it entirely to Johnston as the head of the department. Seddon wished to give Johnston a chance to invigorate the enfeebled cause of the West, but he reckoned without Johnston's eccentricity and unwillingness to take the chance. At one point in Johnston's controversy with the War Department, he asserted that to take Bragg's army away from him would be "inconsistent with his personal honor."

Davis has been blamed for the blunders in the West, and he must take his share of the blame, but Johnston's share, in 1863, was by far the larger. Davis had washed his hands of the problem of Bragg, and left it solely up to the commander of the department; it was not his fault that Johnston persisted in praising a man whom all men knew to be incompetent. Davis could not afford to overstep Johnston's opinion and remove Bragg, even had he desired to do so, for Bragg would have had only too just a reason for complaint. Johnston, however, was suffering from his old wound, and we shall never know just how unfit he was for active service. The mystery, the wholly inexplicable part of Johnston's conduct, was not so much his own dislike of taking the field; it was his refusal to let anybody else take Bragg's place.

As the spring advanced and Grant's maneuvers around Vicksburg grew more menacing, the Army of Mississippi, commanded by General John C. Pemberton, became the strategic center of the war, because control of the "Father of Waters" was indispensable to the ultimate success of either side. Pemberton, another favorite of the President, was even more incompetent than Bragg. But he was not so great a favorite, and Johnston certainly had the authority to remove him. Davis has been misjudged; it has been said that he should have removed Bragg and, particularly, Pemberton, but it is forgotten that Johnston constantly defended them both. Davis was simply failing to do what he has so often been charged with doing—overruling a commander on the scene of action. He took Johnston at his word. This word was not unequivocal; Johnston, in March, congratulated Pemberton on the skill of his operation against Grant, presumably because he himself was glad that he was not engaging in operations against anybody; yet his opinion of Pemberton, expressed later, was actually very low. Seddon, and Davis, too, had pleaded with

Johnston time and again to take command at Vicksburg in person; he invariably gave his excuse—illness.

Johnston complained—much more plausiby—that both of the armies in his department were too small to keep back the enemy and to reinforce each other, and he kept demanding troops from the west side of the Mississippi that were either idle or much nearer Pemberton than Bragg, who was off in Tennessee. But Davis, faced with the most critical of disasters, would not violate the highly unnatural boundary of a department, and the troops from the Trans-Mississippi never came.

In spite of the lack of effective leadership for all the armies, the outlook for the spring of 1863 seemed to be better than it had been the year before. In the whole theater of war the Federals had not gained ground since April, 1862; indeed, they had lost a little. Richmond was safe, and the Confederates had reestablished a foothold in Tennessee; Arkansas was still disputed ground, although Missouri was gone forever. The Southern armies were larger, better equipped, and, on the whole, better officered. To offset these advantages, the troops were scattered.

The country, besides, had been restless all winter, and the government did not know how to get what it wanted without ruffling the feelings of the people. Confederate money was going to the bad; merchants began to refuse it. Food became hard to get, though there was an increasing plenty of it. The railroads were breaking down under the strain of war; materials of upkeep, hitherto imported from the North, could not be replaced. The government now resorted to a tax in kind, an impressment of farm produce for the Army; the farmers retaliated by raising only enough for home use. The planters were urged to leave off growing tobacco and cotton and to grow foodstuffs. Toombs was enraged at this interference from the central government and planted his usual amount of cotton. The government agencies of all kinds were feebly organized and administered—the Southerners were not good businessmen—and the public, unlike the modern Americans, was fiercely opposed to all forms of outside control. A magnetic leader might have cajoled the Southern people into even greater sacrifices than those they made spontaneously, but Davis could not spare the time from the duties of a commander of many armies. The Lower South, the heart of the Southern movement, began to feel that it was ignored.

In Virginia, after the Battle of Fredericksburg, Lee had gone to Richmond, where he was assured by the President that the end of the war was in sight. The slaughter of the Union troops in that struggle had greatly depressed the North, for though in the fall the invasions of Maryland and Kentucky had failed, the Union had not won a victory in the field since Shiloh, nine months before. But the winter passed. Lincoln kept up the war, and Europe did nothing to stop it.

By April, 1863, the situation in Virginia, though more hopeful than it had been the year before, was difficult. A large detachment from Lee's army under General James Longstreet was off in Suffolk, uselessly besieging that town and gathering supplies for the main army. The expedition was a concession to the Confederate commissary to which Lee unwisely consented; it left Lee with barely 60,000 men to oppose about 113,000, "the finest army on this planet," under General Joseph Hooker, who had replaced Burnside and reorganized his army. The two armies still faced each other on the Rappahannock at Fredericksburg, and Hooker was to advance upon Richmond, while Grant, performing his part of the grand strategy, captured Vicksburg. On the last day of April, Hooker started to move; his plan was to hold Lee's army at Fredericksburg with about half of his own, which was nearly equal to the whole of Lee's, and with the other half, march to Lee's rear, cut off his retreat to Richmond, and crush him as in a vise. The plan was perfect—on paper; but it took no account of Lee and Jackson.

They quickly upset Hooker's plan by taking the offensive themselves, bringing on the Battle of Chancellorsville. Leaving only a small detachment to feint at Fredericksburg, they marched eighteen miles westward to meet Hooker in the famous and difficult Spotsylvania wilderness. In the presence of 70,000 men, Lee divided his fewer than 50,000 and on May 2 sent Jackson to the right flank and rear of Hooker. Jackson, at the height of his career, moved like lightning upon Hooker, crushed his right wing, and routed it. Night came on, and Jackson fell, mortally wounded by his own men in the tangled woods.

In the next two days Lee completed the victory, which has been called the tactical masterpiece of the nineteenth century. But victory was not the destruction which Jackson was at the point of achieving, and the Federal Army retreated, soon to be as powerful as ever. Yet the Federal offensive in the East had been thrown back, and the Confederates had the initiative. It remained to see what they would be able to do with it.

Not only was the loss of Jackson irreparable; it made the next campaign, unwisely conceived, sure to fail. The Battle of Chancellorsville, triumph that it was, eliminated Jackson and made inevitable, because the triumph was partial, the invasion of Pennsylvania. Lee could not afford to let the upper hand go unimproved, and he drew to his support the main attention of the War Department, while the vastly more important problem of Vicksburg was left to its own solution.

In the middle of May, Davis gave his consent to the Northern invasion, but four days later he heard of Pemberton's defeat and his flight to Vicksburg. Grant's army had looted Brierfield, and Grant himself was riding one of the famous Davis horses. Because he had confidence in Lee's ultimate success, Davis had patriotically sacrificed his own interest and his own people. The news from Pemberton, however, called for consideration, and on May 26 Davis convened the most momentous Cabinet meeting in the history of the Confederacy. All day and into the night the members of the Cabinet discussed the military crisis.

Davis, ill, tired, austere, said little. Benjamin entered suavely into the talk; Memminger, who knew nothing of war, looked nervous and out of place; Mallory had little to say. Seddon led the discussion, opposed by Reagan, the Postmaster General from the West, who argued passionately for the defense of Vicksburg. But the Cabinet had already made up its mind to support Lee and to stake everything on Lee's invasion of the North. Until a few weeks before, Seddon had continued to support Johnston's demands from the West. But now Chancellorsville had changed the outlook; defensive war had failed, and at last here was the chance for an overwhelming offensive, which should have been undertaken in 1861. Lee was more powerful than he had been after Second Manassas. Everywhere, in spite of the siege of Vicksburg, the Confederate hope was high, and in spite of deficient strategy, there was a great chance for success.

The Confederacy, truly medieval in war, as it was feudal in society, had blind faith in the value of capitals, of fortified cities. Lee believed that his march to Pennsylvania would force Grant to send men from his army to the East. Not a man came.

Early in June, Lee set his army in motion for the Shenandoah Valley in order to enter Pennsylvania west of the Blue Ridge, a barrier between him and the Union Army. Since the death of Jackson the Army of Northern Virginia had been reorganized in three corps under Generals Longstreet, Richard Ewell, and Ambrose Hill, for Lee was not willing to trust a new officer with as large a body of men as Jackson had commanded.

While the army was moving, there occurred a great cavalry battle at Brandy Station, Virginia, on June 9; it ended drawn, and the result was ominous. It meant that Jeb Stuart's cavalry was no longer definitely superior to the Union's. As the war progressed the Union troops of all arms steadily improved, and the initial superior aptitude of the Confederates for war was an advantage that had been lost. The Army of the Potomac, but for leadership and organization, was now very nearly the equal of Lee's, and its superior numbers, not important up to this time, were beginning to be decisive.

In the last days of June, Lee's army was in Pennsylvania; Ewell had advanced as far as York and threatened Harrisburg. Davis had failed to form a "skeleton army" between Richmond and Washington, as Lee had requested, because there was no available men in that department; Richmond might have been taken by a forceful attack, but it was not. Davis, terribly anxious, tried to believe the hopeful dispatches from Vicksburg; an a momentary panic he warned

Lee not to go too far away, then took the warning back. The absence of the "skeleton army" relieved Lincoln of anxiety for Washington and permitted him to send the whole of Hooker's army after Lee. Hooker followed closely, but Lee, having permitted Stuart to indulge in a wild raid, knew little of the position of the Union Army.

The first clash at Gettysburg was unforeseen, but by nightfall of July 1 it was obvious that a great battle could not be avoided. Lee had preferred to fight in the mountains, on the defensive; Longstreet had insisted upon it. But the advantage gained on July 1, when two Federal corps were practically destroyed, made Lee decide to follow up the first success. The Union Army was strung out over thirty miles, while Lee's was concentrated; he had, for the first time in the war, the opportunity to oppose smaller numbers. Longstreet was therefore ordered to crush the Union left flank at dawn of July 2. He argued and delayed till three-thirty that afternoon, when he had opposed to him a new Federal corps just arrived on the field; even at that he almost broke the Federal line.

Next day, partial success having been won, Lee determined to try again, though now his army of 75,000 men was opposed by the whole Federal army of 93,000 under General George Gordon Meade, a fine soldier, who at the last moment had superseded Hooker. Again Lee ordered the attack to begin at dawn; again Longstreet, convinced it would fall, ensured its failure by putting off the attack till after three o'clock. This attack, known as Pickett's charge, was preceded by a tremendous artillery battle; and then the 14,000 Confederates—without support, though it was supposed to be there—marched with iron ranks across a mile of open ground through a veritable hell of musketry and canister shot. They captured the first line and came so near success that 5,000 more men would have made it certain. Then at the critical moment the unsupported victors were overwhelmed. Lee has been blamed for taking such a great chance—the risk was enormous—and yet it is clear that the task was by no means impossible if ably carried out. Longstreet had simply flouted his orders. Lee had got used to Jackson, whose aggressive genius was eminently suited to the needs of Gettysburg. Lee said afterward, "If I had had Stonewall Jackson at Gettysburg, I should have won a great victory."

If Lee's army had been larger and better supplied, he need not have returned to Virginia, for Meade had merely fought him to a standstill, and he was too weak to resume the campaign so far from his base. The victory for the Union was not tactical and overwhelming, as Union patriotism to this day makes it out to have been, but strategic. Meade, in fact, had been so badly shattered in holding his own that, like McClellan, he pursued Lee at a distance and did not assume the offensive for the rest of the year. Late in the summer, Lee himself became the aggressor again, but Meade maneuvered and did not fight.

Nevertheless, the Pennsylvania campaign, because

Lee was compelled to retreat, was a dire disaster. On July 4, the day Lee started back to Virginia, Vicksburg fell at last, with a loss of 29,000 men. Defeated both East and West, the South now entered upon a new phase, in which the offensive would never again be possible.

The lull between battles in the East gave the Confederate Government time to reorganize the forces of the West, and at the suggestion of General Polk, Johnston's small army was united with Bragg's in Tennessee. Grant, fortunately for the Confederates, took no decisive action. His army was broken up into garrison detachments along the Mississippi, as if the Federals were well enough contented with their great victory to rest upon it for a time. Rosecrans, facing Bragg, was hardly more enterprising than his opponent; he took no advantage of Grant's victory, and Lincoln was as deeply annoyed with his lack of energy as Davis was with Johnston's. Not all but something might be recovered if Rosecrans could be crushed, and Davis at last got Lee's consent to transfer part of his army to Bragg for temporary service. This was the first time in three years of war that the South used the interior lines for the swift transfer of troops from one center of war to another, and it was probably now too late to use this advantage effectively. In the middle of September, Bragg was prodded into taking the offensive, having been driven from Chattanooga without a battle, and Longstreet's corps started from Virginia.

In the week following September 10 hardly a day passed that did not offer to Bragg the opportunity to crush Rosecrans' scattered army in detail. But he seems, during this time, to have had only vague ideas where the enemy was; he was not certain from day to day of the position of his own troops. When Longstreet arrived (almost too late), he was shocked at the methods he saw. He described Bragg's strategy—"To wait till all good opportunities had passed, and then, in description, to seize upon the least favorable one." With Longstreet's corps, Bragg now had 70,000 men to attack Rosecrans' 57,000—the only time the Confederates outnumbered all the available enemy on the field.

The savage and reckless Battle of Chickamauga was fought on September 19 and 20, 1863, but Bragg was not even on the field; he knew, in his panic, so little of the position of the enemy and of the dispositions of his own men that his orders were wild and impossible to carry out. Longstreet directed the battle, and for the first time in the war the Western Confederate armies had able leadership. The Confederates by sheer valor drove the Federals back, till finally Longstreet discovered a gap in their line and cut it in two. Had not the Union General George Thomas held on with a remnant till night, the Federal Army would have been annihilated. As it was, much was accomplished with a hitherto demoralized army, because an officer of great ability—not even of the greatest—had controlled the field. However, the victory was thrown away, for Bragg, instead of pursuing Rosecrans, waited a day, and found the Union Army entrenched in Chattanooga. He then dismissed General Polk, whom he hated, and General Daniel H. Hill, of Longstreet's corps; he blamed the incomplete victory on them. Hill, who had ignored Bragg's orders only because they were incoherent, was the instigator of a scheme to get rid of Bragg. Davis restored Polk, but permitted Hill, one of the heroes of Sharpsburg and a distinguished soldier, to be disgraced.

The President was much pleased at the victory, but he was dissatisfied that it had not been complete. He was utterly bewildered at the continued unpopularity of Bragg, in whom he supposed victory would restore confidence.

He retained Bragg. The retention of Bragg was an act of madness, because the Army of Tennessee became its sacrifice. He could be retained only at the expense of the loss of Longstreet, who openly and contemptuously said that he would not serve under him. Davis therefore sent Longstreet with 20,000 men on a futile expedition against Knoxville, reducing Bragg's army and exposing it to inevitable defeat. Nor was the mere loss in men the most serious loss; when Longstreet disappeared, the morale of the army disappeared, too.

For a few weeks after Chickamauga it seemed that

Bragg would be able to starve Rosecrans, penned up in Chattanooga, into surrender. The Union supplies came over a bad road sixty miles long, for Bragg held every other access. But Grant soon came on the scene, and the situation changed. He opened a new route of supply, and by the third week in November he was ready to take the offensive. Bragg held the surrounding mountains; his position looked impregnable. As it turned out, it was never really decided whether it was. For at the first onslaught of Grant's army—Rosecrans having been relieved—the Confederates turned and fled.

It was the first time a Confederate army had offered its back to the enemy; this army, moreover, had fought with desperation only two months before. It was demoralized before the first shot of the Battle of Chattanooga. The men simply laid down their arms and ran.

Anger, fierce and relentless, swept over the whole South, and from this time on, Davis lost utterly the confidence of the Southern people. Not only the fire-eating leaders, but the common people, who bore the brunt of the war, turned against the Davis government. If folly had ended even here, there might have been some hope of winning back the affections of the people. But it did not end. Bragg was not immediately dismissed. Davis still made excuses.

Davis, defiant of popular dictation, made Braxton Bragg chief of staff of the Confederate armies—the post that Lee had held in 1862. Bragg would have powerful influence in the war policy of the South, and the public now felt that Davis was indeed a tyrant. He was only proud and obstinate. Nevertheless, men whispered that his Western journey had been the first step to a dictatorship.

7 The Death Struggle: 1864

THE ELEVATION of Bragg to his new post of honor met bitter opposition, for his popular following in Virginia was even scantier than in the West. Congress, led by Wigfall and Orr, wrangled with Davis over the question of his pay. The salary of Bragg was not the real issue, but Davis could not see it. The issue was the President himself.

Memminger came in for his share of abuse, and he resigned, leaving the finances of the South in a hopeless tangle. The Treasury no longer knew how much paper had been issued; there was nothing that even a money wizard could have done.

Most ominous of all, Congress passed a resolution complimenting Lee, which grew at last, under the agitation of Henry S. Foote, into a plot to make Lee dictator. Lee, of course, would not consider the proposal. But Davis would have been wise to make him

135

commander in chief before it was too late; he was willing to give him the place—in fact, he approached him with the offer—but with conditions. Davis still wished to be commander in chief in name; he could not bring himself to admit that he was a military failure. Lee had all he could do to keep one army supplied, without taking vague responsibility for armies elsewhere, and the farthest he would go was to give indefinite, if sound, advice.

Davis was now trying heroically to harmonize all the warring parties; the task was formidable, but there was still some reasonable hope of success. However, the social and political scene in the first months of 1864 was quickly moving from the confusion of 1863 into chaos. The Confederacy was cut in two and had been since Vicksburg, though none but the wisest understood how serious this was.

The authority of the government at Richmond reached only a fraction of the South. A line drawn from Lee's army on the Rapidan in Virginia, through the southwestern part of that state, down to Dalton, Georgia, not far from Chattanooga, thence jaggedly to Mobile, Alabama, encloses the territory that, in early 1864, was under Confederate protection. All of Mississippi was gone, most of Alabama. But because this whole line was not visibly manned every few yards by Federal soldiers, the Mississippians and Alabamans clung to their hope—complaining, however, that they were expected to give men and supplies to a government that could not give them protection from Federal marauders in return.

Disaffection grew into disloyalty. There were mumblings for peace. In 1863 Governor Zebulon Vance of North Carolina, doubtless regretting the long interval between undisturbed drinks with the governor of South Carolina, suggested that Davis start peace negotiations. This was the beginning of a delusion that the Southern states could return to the Union at will and on their own terms. By the end of 1862 the character of the war had changed. The North had begun with the denial of states' rights and proceeded to a war of conquest; the South had begun with the defense of states' rights but necessarily moved into a war for independence or nothing. The doctrinaire states' rightists, of course, were not aware of this, because they still supposed that people poured out their blood for abstractions.

In North Carolina the slogan was: "The Constitution as it is and the Union as it was." This was the sentiment of the small farmers who, having had little experience in society and national politics, imagined that even now, after three years of bloodletting, it was not too late to remove differences with talk. But Vance himself became so alarmed at the more violent position of W. W. Holden, his rival for the governorship, that, when reelected, he never mentioned unvictorious peace again. However, he did not support the central government; his unflagging aim was to cripple conscription, and he constantly baited the people with the assertion

137

that poor North Carolina was being trampled on in the interests of the other states. He opened his resources only to North Carolina regiments; in March, 1865, he had in his warehouses about 95,000 new Confederate uniforms, while the Army of Northern Virginia was in rags, and enough rations, when it was starving, to feed it for three or four months. The Confederacy starved, but not because of the lack of food.

The belligerent and outspoken Holden was a most ominous sign. He was the respectable political representative of a sentiment not always so respectable. He said, "If the people of North Carolina are for perpetual conscriptions, impressments and seizures to keep up a perpetual, devastating and exhausting war, let them vote for Governor Vance." At his back roamed, in the mountains and swamps, hordes of armed deserters, unwilling conscripts, men who had little interest in the war and resented outside control. They gathered in bands and preyed on the defenseless districts where the manpower was in the Army, attacked the helpless Negro, whom they hated because he was the instrument of their own neglect under the planter regime; in the mountains they murdered Negroes and whites alike. At one place they numbered 500 men in an entrenched camp. These gangs pillaged farms and villages in all the upland districts—North Carolina, southwestern Virginia, north Georgia, north Alabama, east Tennessee.

Such were the extreme signs of discontent. That the

138

more respectable and loyal portion, the majority of the Southern people, were restless could not be denied, and Davis asked the new Congress, their restless representatives, for strong measures to bring the people to order. In the end, it is doubtful if Davis, using all the tricks of the demagogue, could have conciliated such fantastic opposition to carrying on the war—for that was what it amounted to.

Nevertheless, the Confederate Government had powerful armies in the field for the 1864 campaign. The chief difficulty was feeding them; there was food, but the transportation system was worse than ever. The equipment of the armies was better than it had ever been. The armies, East and West, were armed with the finest Enfield rifles; and the Tredegar Ironworks in Richmond could now cast the best of ordnance. There were arsenals and munitions plants at Selma, Alabama, at Atlanta, Georgia, at Fayetteville, North Carolina. Davis could boast that he had established the finest powder mill in the world.

There was reason to expect success, not only becaus the armies were still kept up, but because the North was about to have acute troubles of her own. As the winter passed into spring, Davis, who had listened first to Lee, then to Seddon, and was now hearing the soothing voice of Bragg, had decided to undertake a powerful offensive against Sherman, who had succeeded Grant in the command of the West. It was dangerous strategy for a man not naturally bold.

The armies were still powerful, but losses inevitable

in another campaign could not be replaced: the manpower, as 1864 opened, was practically exhausted—the available manpower, for the deserters and skulkers could not be counted.

Davis now consented to let Bragg push Johnston into an offensive—the decision of a losing gambler, cornered. It was the first time that he had heartily approved of offensive strategy; when it had had chance of success, he had supported it with a divided mind and coined the phrase "offensive defensive." Lee's invasion of Pennsylvania had been crippled by the retention of small garrisons along the coast and in the interior; it was a combination, fatal to complete success, of offensive and defensive strategy that, because of the limited resources of men, was bound to fail if the Army of the Potomac was competently led. There is little doubt that Lee, with 100,000 men and in spite of Longstreet's mistakes, would have demolished Meade's army at Gettysburg. He should have been given that number for an overwhelming offensive, or the offensive should not have been launched at all.

As early as February, Bragg began urging Johnston to advance when spring came, into Tennessee, with an army that he himself had left demoralized. Johnston did not approve of the plan, nor did Longstreet, who was still in east Tennessee. Bragg wanted to give Longstreet to Johnston, but Longstreet soon rejoined Lee on the Rapidan. However, every effort was made to strengthen Johnston's army, so that when the campaign opened, he mustered about 65,000 men—more than Lee had. But he was opposed by Sherman, the ablest fighting general of the Union, with 100,000. Davis seems to have left the whole matter to Bragg, and it can hardly be doubted that Bragg misrepresented to Davis the Western situation. He exaggerated Johnston's numbers and resources, and he minimized the strength of Sherman—perhaps not consciously, but because he was impelled by the demands of a weak and hysterical nature to believe what he wished to believe in his own self-vindication. Davis was neither weak nor hysterical, but he was desperate, and he was willing to listen to hopeful words from whatever source they might come, even from a general who had been a failure in every field.

The days of March and April were full of anxiety, and the President's poor health was at its worst. He still worked doggedly at his military details—shoes for this brigade, the appointment of a surgeon to that—but he was more affable than he had ever been before. He continued his daily horseback rides. Then, to his terrible anxiety for public affairs were added the effects of private grief. Mrs. Davis at this time was in the habit of bringing him his lunch to his office, and one day, while they were together at the luncheon hour, an excited Negro ran in with the news that their little boy, Joseph Emory Davis, had fallen off a gallery. When the parents got to him, he was dead.

A messenger arrived with a dispatch; Davis said, "I must have this day with my little child." He was prostrated, and he repeated again and again, " 'Not mine, O Lord, but Thine.' " Next day his powerful will had steadied him, and he kept his office hours.

The campaign of 1864 opened, not in the West, but in Virginia, and more fiercely than ever before. Grant, after his victory at Chattanooga, had been made a lieutenant general in command of all the armies of the Union, and he proceeded to formulate the grand strategic plan which, if successful, would put an end to the Confederacy forever. General Butler's army on the peninsula below Richmond formed the Union left; Meade's Army of the Potomac, north of the Rapidan, which Grant decided to command in person, was the center; Sherman's army in northern Georgia was the right. They were to move simultaneously as one great army, and to crush the South. By this time Lincoln had stopped playing the game of war, and the credit for the Union strategy belongs solely to Grant. His own object was Lee's army and Richmond; General William Sherman's, Johnston and the capture of Atlanta. If these ends could be achieved, the Confederacy would fall.

In the first days of May, Grant crossed the Rapidan River with 120,000 men. He had expected to be opposed, and when he saw that Lee did not dispute the crossing, he marched confidently into the Spotsylvania wilderness, intending to clear it and attack Lee in the open ground on the south side. Lee, with 60,000, fell like a thunderbolt on Grant while he was still entangled in the thicket; Grant's superior numbers, unwieldy in the brush, were largely neutralized, and his artillery could not be used. The dismal and bloody Battle of the Wilderness, was a tactical victory for Lee; he rolled up both flanks of the Union Army, just as Jackson, the year before, had crushed the right flank of Hooker's troops; but he lacked the reserve power to make the victory decisive. But Grant, who was a very different man from Hooker, was not demoralized and did not give up the field, though his losses had been terrific and two corps of the Union Army practically destroyed. He then decided on "fight[ing] it out on this line, if it takes all summer," for his losses could, unlike Lee's, be replaced, until in the end he thought the South would have to yield.

Any of the generals who had preceded Grant would surely have retreated, but baffled as he was, he gave the order, "Forward, by the left flank," and the Army of the Potomac moved to the southeast toward Spotsylvania Courthouse, near Richmond. Lee said to his staff, "Gentlemen, the Army of the Potomac at last has a head." But Lee again foiled his enemy by winning the race to Spotsylvania, and Grant found him entrenched and formidable as ever. Grant was outgeneraled, and all he could do was hurl his men against Lee in frontal attacks. At Spotsylvania he gained, at the famous Bloody Angle, a momentary success, but in the end he was repulsed. The slaughter—it was literally that—was unspeakable; for the first time the trenches literally ran with blood, and special details were constantly removing the bodies so that the men

143

could fight without standing upon them. Baffled again, Grant again sidled toward Richmond, and found Lee too strongly entrenched on the North Anna to attack him; once more he sidled and then fought the Battle of Cold Harbor, the scene of the struggle of Gaines' Mill in 1862.

Grant, knowing no tactics but headlong attack, now precipitated the most useless butchery of men in American history. By this time he was desperate; the whole North was looking on, and he had not yet whipped "Bobby" Lee. The Federal privates had begun saying, "No matter who the general is, he can't whip Bobby Lee." He ordered a frontal attack all along the line, and Lee's men, behind earthworks, shot down 8,000 in half an hour, while only a few hundred Confederates fell. It is said that Grant threw himself on an Army cot and wept, and yet he ordered another attack; it is the only time that Grant became unnerved. The Federal soldiers would not move; it was a passive mutiny that Grant could not ignore, and he abandoned the attack. Still, he would not admit defeat. The wounded Federals lay for twenty-four hours between the lines. This was the darkest hour of Grant's career, for instead of acknowledging defeat and asking for a truce, he disingenuously accused Lee, in a note, of responsibility for the sufferings of the wounded Federals. At Cold Harbor the two armies faced each other for some days.

Davis was again constantly at the front, although now he was giving less advice than ever to Lee. His greatest anxiety was the safety of Petersburg, threatened by Butler, and he held frequent conferences with Beauregard, who commanded that department. Beauregard proposed, while Lee and Grant hesitated after Cold Harbor, to transfer part of Lee's army to reinforce his own small force so that Butler could be destroyed, then to rejoin Lee for an effective blow against Grant. Who can say that the plan would not have succeeded? However, it called forth from Lee the only curt and peremptroy letter on record; he warned Beauregard that unless he sent more troops speedily to the Army of Northern Virginia, the result would be disaster. Butler blundered and did not take Petersburg. Grant began his turning movement again, crossing the James, and by the end of June the siege of Petersburg began.

Davis was once more confident that all chances of success were not gone. There was ground for the confidence, but he did not suppose that victory was near. One day, walking in the public square by the capitol, he talked to some young girls, who asked, in reply to his confident words, "But shall the Army be fed?" The President answered, "I don't see why rats, if fat, are not as good as squirrels."

Rats, however, were not Davis' hope for the Confederacy, but the fact that Lee had fought the greatest of his campaigns and that Grant's failure to complete his part of the Federal grand strategy had almost demoralized the Northern people. Lee had been outnumbered in all the battles since the first of May—

the Wilderness, Spotsylvania, Cold Harbor—exactly two to one; although at the end, if Grant had received no reinforcements, their number would have been about equal, for Lee had put on his back nearly as many men as he had in his own army at the beginning of the campaign. Grant had lost, without having visibly achieved more than McClellan in 1862, who had arrived before Richmond with a trifling loss. He lost 60,000 men and won for himself the name "Butcher Grant." A moan of horror and despair swept the whole North, and Davis now began to look in that direction, as he had previously looked to Europe, for assistance to end the war.

The Northern people were not aware that Grant's policy of attrition was gradually wearing out the Confederates; they knew only that he had not taken Richmond and that he was sending their sons to slaughter.

Davis was doing his utmost to profit by the Northern panic. In July he brought upon himself the renewed wrath of his enemies—Lee by this time was given sole credit for every success—by receiving unaccredited emissaries from the North, who came talking peace. Their motive is to this day not quite clear; probably Lincoln wished to sound out the Confederate morale, to see how far the Confederate leaders despaired of success. Davis' reception was not official; he met the two men informally in Benjamin's office. They were naïvely surprised at his consistent reference to the "two countries" and at his unwillingness to consider re-

146

union. Then they departed as mysteriously as they came.

The history of Jefferson Davis during the War Between the States is practically identical with the movements, the failures, and the victories of the Southern armies. He had almost no social life, and his political life was the shadow of his military policy. The vast drama of the war in a sense the externalization of the interior drama of Davis' soul. Every event was swiftly and subtly, sometimes tortuously, recoreded upon his sensibility, and the marches of armies and the tactics of battles were the reflections of his own powerful will.

When Grant crossed the Rapidan, Sherman marched against Johnston in Georgia. Johnston began falling back, slowly and carefully, before Sherman's greater strength. An offensive was out of the question, and Johnston knew it, for he would have done well to preserve his army intact on the defensive. Bragg, at the outset of the campaign, had Johnston where he wanted him; he was convinced that Johnston would not throw himself headlong against Sherman, and he was equally certain, since the President was of the belief that Johnston had the strength, that this would mean his rival's fall. For he had argued the President into the lulling belief that this was the hour for aggression.

Johnston continued to fall back all through May before the finest army in America; it was probably the finest, best-drilled, and best-equipped army in the world, commanded by a general whose military genius was as great as his personal integrity as a man was small.

Toward the end of May, Johnston has decided that there was only one way to thwart Sherman. It was impossible to betray so clever a soldier into a frontal attack on the Confederate works; Sherman, unlike Grant, moved around the Confederate flank without fighting, advancing a little each day. The solution to the problem was suggested by Nathan Bedford Forrest, who, as early as April, advised Johnston to send him against Sherman's communications with 10,000 cavalry. Sherman would in this fashion, be cut off from his supplies, and in the mountains of Georgia he would find little provender and be forced to retreat or attack Johnston's entrenchments. If he did the latter, he would be almost certain to be hurled back and defeated. In this terrible crisis the South had for its salvation the heaven-sent genius of Forrest, one of the greatest cavalry leaders of modern times, and it only remained to be seen whether Davis would use him and be saved.

From May until July, Johnston patiently and persistently pleaded with Davis through Bragg to send Forrest against Sherman's line of supply. Again and again, the plea was rejected. Bragg, with an omniscient air, replied once that the movement had been considered, then changed the subject.

So Johnston's retreat, which day by day let Sherman get nearer Atlanta, inevitably continued, but still the

President kept the wires hot, demanding why Sherman was not attacked.

Most of Bragg's misinformation came from General John B. Hood, a gallant subordinate who had the brain of a hare and the personal courage of a lion. Hood, in fact, was Bragg's choice as Johnston's successor; he was honestly impatient with Johnston's cautious retreat, and he may have been infatuated with the prospect of conducting a dashing campaign that would save the Confederacy. It is impossible to believe that Hood was not an honest man; he was the tool of Bragg and of fate.

Before Davis would consent to Hood's promotion, he asked Lee what he thought of him. (Hood had commanded a division under Lee.) Lee replied cautiously yet unmistakably that Hood was brave and zealous but implied that he should not command an army. The excited and desperate mind of Davis was no longer sensitive to innuendo, and he seems to have thought that Lee had confirmed the choice. Lee's disapproval really shouts from the page. The truth was that Davis had made up his mind, and he was now capable of hearing only those words that he wished to hear.

As Johnston fell back steadily the Georgia country people began complaining, although he still had the full confidence of his army. For the first, and perhaps the last time, Jefferson Davis heeded what the frightened populace said; it confirmed his belief that Johnston should be removed. Johnston had to go.

Bragg succeeded in removing his enemy, just as his enemy, according to his own statement—and Johnston was too honorable to lie—was planning to deliver Sherman a blow. Joseph E. Johnston, whose limitations are well-known, was a fine soldier and a true patriot; he wept in regret for the fatal step Davis had taken, but he spoke not a word in detraction of General Hood.

In spite of public opinion, Bragg had virtually resumed command in the West; Hood was his tool. Together they planned a series of attacks on Sherman's entrenchments, and on July 22 they drove some of Sherman's men back, but at frightful loss. Bragg informed Davis that Sherman "was badly defeated and completely failed in one of his turning movements, heretofore so successful." He could gloat over his rival's fall for a time, but by the end of August Sherman had got in the rear of Atlanta, after defeating Hood in several pitched battles, and Hood had to retreat. On September 2 Atlanta fell. Thus ended Bragg's brilliant offensive in the West, and at this moment the Confederacy was beaten.

Atlanta was the strategic center of the Confederacy, for it opened all of Georgia to Sherman, who could now march through the heart of the country and circle around to the rear of Lee's army at Petersburg. But even more important at the moment was the effect that the fall of Atlanta had on the Northern people. The victory had restored prestige to the Lincoln government, and he was certain to be elected in November. The war, two months before on the point of collapse, would be pushed by the North to the end.

8 Revolution and Collapse

THE CONFEDERACY now became a vast stage, with Davis occupying the center, and every event was a harbinger of disaster. The news of Hood's defeat and the loss of Atlanta came to Davis, in spite of the ease with which even ordinary men had predicted them, as a crushing surprise; all the beautiful plans spun for him by his friend Bragg had toppled like a house of cards—for such they were. He was now utterly discredited, and the few friends he had left were discredited with him; the people had lost faith in Davis and all his works. The mutterings of the summer had turned into howls of rage.

Now clearly, but not for the first time, the pedantic folly of the Montgomery Convention of 1861 bore fruit; it had set up for six years a government that could not be removed without resorting to revolution. The disaffection of the people after September, 1864, has been interpreted as disgust with the war and desire for the old Union, but except for some feeling of this kind in a few places, the dissatisfaction was not with the war, but with the Davis government. Revolution was in the air, and Governor Joseph Brown of Georgia was helping to plot it. He shouted that his noble state would fight the South and the North together to preserve her rights.

By the middle of September, Brown resumed his carping, quibbling, obstructing controversy with Davis, in defense of what he supposed to be states' rights. Now that Hood was defeated and the need for men was all the greater, he promptly recalled about 10,000 Georgia militiamen who were serving with the main army; he feared they would be taken from Georgia soil.

Sherman was so encouraged by the anti-Davis agitation of Brown and of Stephens (who still believed that violation of the Constitution had brought all the recent disasters) that he tried to open peace negotiations with them for the surrender of Georgia. It came to nothing, but Brown afterwards wrote to Stephens that "it keeps the door open," and one can only surmise that Brown's ignorant hysteria and Stephen's doctrinaire fanaticism had led them to the verge of treason.

An example of the absolute power that Davis aimed at was the attempt of the Confederate Government to regulate food prices and to protect the public from the extortionists, who were making 400 percent or more. This was bitterly opposed, even by the people who were being robbed, as a usurpation of the central government! Governor William Smith of Virginia, finding that rice sold in the market at two dollars and fifty cents a pound, bought up rice and offered it to the public at fifty cents, which included a profit. However, Smith was attacked by the Constitutional fiddlers at the burning of the Confederate Rome. The regulation of prices was an invasion of states' rights, the iron policy of ambitious politicians, "men whose ambitious designs," in the words of the Georgia peace resolutions of 1864, "would need cover under the ever-recurring plea of the necessities of war." Stephens justified his part in the peace resolutions on the ground that they would work against Lincoln's reelection, making a "deep impression upon the minds of all true friends of Constitutional liberty" in the North. As if the people North or South at the moment cared a fig for anything but victory in the war!

Against this background of dissention, cross-purpose, recrimination, and despair, Jefferson Davis began acting out his part in the last scene of a drama, not of his own choice, but, as we have seen, largely of his making. The drama was moving swiftly to its end. On September 28, 1864, President Davis arrived unexpectedly at Macon, Georgia, for the last time to appeal to the people of the West and to direct the Army to victory.

This, Davis' third and final visit to the West, was attended everywhere by the most discouraging signs.

As always, his chief concern was the Army. He held long and repeated conferences with Hood. What could be done? He could hardly have believed at this time that Hood was the general to conduct a successful campaign against Sherman, for he virtually admitted his loss of faith by appointing the still-popular Beauregard to the command of the department, in which position Beauregard nominally outranked Hood. Hood himself was aware that he had been a failure, and he offered to resign. Here Davis had a perfect opportunity to dispose of him without doing violence to his own pride, but he would not seize it. He had elevated Hood, and he was too stubborn to admit his mistake; if the public had favored Hood, he might have removed him, but he would not let opposition dictate to him. Again, he did not know what to do beyond the harrowing awareness that something must be done. In Hood's camp the men cried out, "Give us General Johnston!"

Davis wished Hood to fight a battle on the Georgia-Tennessee border, having at last adopted Johnston's strategy of falling on Sherman's communications. Hood was to march north in the belief that Sherman would be compelled to follow him, and thus Georgia would be relieved. Unfortunately, Davis, trying to re-animate the people, announced the plan to Sherman, who until then had been in some doubt as to what he should do. Davis' speech was immediately put in Sherman's hands.

At last, after Atlanta was already lost, Forrest's plan was adopted. Hood marched north, tearing up

Sherman's railroad communications, and expected Sherman to pursue him. This Sherman did—at a distance; then he decided to ignore Hood and continue his march through Georgia. Before him now lay the low country, the granary of the Confederacy, and he no longer needed his line of supplies; he could easily reach Savannah and the Federal fleet, living meanwhile on the country. The world knows how well he accomplished this. Hood's action was simply insane —a defeated army marching into territory held by the enemy, whose main army was left to its own devices in the rear. Sherman pursued Hood until he saw that Hood would not fight; then he contemptuously turned southward upon his main business.

Hood advanced into Tennessee, hoping that he could defeat the small Union army there under General Thomas. What he hoped beyond this is not known. He was merely striking out blindly. Had he been able to defeat Thomas, he could not have held Tennessee or marched into Kentucky; he was too weak, and inevitable retreat, at the end of which stood Sherman, would have confronted him. Hood was caught between two fires. It had been worse than folly to attempt the forcing of a retreat by Sherman after he was no longer opposed by the main Confederate Army. The situation beautifully illustrated the chief military weakness of Davis; he waited to execute a wise plan until it was too late, for Hood's attempt to break Sherman's communication, under impossible conditions, was suicide. It had not one chance of success.

157

Hood's army, the moment he left Sherman, was, for all effective purposes, extinguished in the West; there was nothing for it to do but disintegrate. The one remaining chance left the South lay in the union of Hood with Lee, who might thus have been able to defeat Grant. This plan was not considered, and there is no way to find out what Davis might have thought of it. It is, however, safe to infer that he could not willingly have brought himself to give up the Western territory, since the mere physical existence of an army there, broken and ill-led though it was, permitted him to cherish the illusion that he could still hold it. At this time he was still appointing generals to departments and keeping up, on paper, the pleasant fiction that they existed.

Hood plunged headlong into Tennessee, toward Nashville. The one great opportunity of the campaign was thrown away. A large part of the Union Army, near Franklin, marched in the night over a road completely commanded by the Confederates, who could hear the tramp of the marching feet. They were permitted merely to listen, and the Federals got away. At Franklin, Hood found them strongly fortified, so he hurled his army against the fortifications. The Confederates won, but at a bloody sacrifice. By the middle of December, Hood was in front of Nashville, with not more than 25,000 men, while Thomas was entrenched with 40,000. Hood, hesitating to attack, sat down before the city and, because he did not know what else to do, waited for Thomas to attack him, which he speedily did. After a fierce but hopeless resistance, the Confederates were driven off with terrible losses, and they fled south to the Tennessee River. In desperately cold weather, half-starving and in rags, the remnant of less than 20,000 doggedly fought off the pursuing Federal cavalry and, after the bitterest hardship, reached Tupelo, Mississippi, in January. The retreat was one of the greatest exploits of the war, for only devotion to the country held together an army wrecked by incompetence and folly. Thus ended the belated strategy which was to frustrate Sherman, who on Christmas Day captured Savannah and started north through the Carolinas like a moving volcano.

Hood resigned, and the news of the disasters in Tennessee conspired with the reports of Sherman's pillage to smite the President at his darkest hour. By December the prospect of certain defeat had made him ill; physically he was a broken man, tortured by neuralgia, stung to the quick by his enemies, perhaps secretly eaten by regret. But on New Year's Day he returned to his office duties, there to pore with fierce intensity over his futile military details. He had no future, no schemes, no hope. Yet he bore himself with all the outward calm of a master of men.

Calmly and regularly, accompanied by his secretary, Burton Harrison, he still rode out to the camps of Lee's army, which was melting away under his eyes. But he had not given up. He was not a great soldier; as President he had been repudiated, but to the end he was, in his own being, a great man.

Sherman's march north through the Carolinas progressed relentlessly, but it was not this that was bringing the South to ruin. It was the lack of a magnetic national leader. The spirit of resistance was not dead; it was paralyzed by distrust of the government. The need of the hour was a revolutionary leader who would call the people to arms, trample on law and government, and conduct a people's war. It is a great mistake to suppose that the South had no chance to win. If ever in history a people fighting for national existence had reason to expect success, those people were the inhabitants of the Southern states.

The South, at the end of 1864, had a great leader whom the people would have followed to the death—Robert E. Lee. The previous agitation to make him dictator now rose to a clamor.

On January 26 Davis signed a bill creating a commander in chief and immediately gave the position to Lee. But that other humiliation, the restoration of Johnston, he would not bear. Lee now used his new authority to order Johnston back to the Western army, and yet he gave not the slightest approval to the anti-Davis movement that had given him the authority. In his reply to Davis he implied a severe rebuke to Davis' enemies: "I am indebted alone to the kindness of His Excellency, the President, for my nomination to this high and arduous office."

Johnston took command of an army mustering not more than 30,000 men, which could only observe the cyclonic Sherman at a safe distance. The promotion of

Lee affected the military policy of the government not at all, for Lee did not assert his authority, and Davis continued to direct. Because Johnston seemed to confront Sherman, the illusion was still possible that the whirlwind was being checked. Not even now was there any real attempt to unite Johnston's army with Lee's at Petersburg.

Davis could not have known how desperate his situation was, yet he knew that it was critical. Late in 1864 the question of arming the slaves came up more urgently than before. Davis, in his overpowering sense of the need to strengthen the armies, from which the deserters numbered 100,000, favored this extreme measure and set about cautiously to get it adopted. If the point were carried, it would be the most revolutionary step of all, for it meant the abolition of slavery.

The variety of prejudice against Negro soldiers was so great that it was almost impossible to frame a policy regarding them that would meet all objections and yet be effective.

Should the Negroes be armed on any condition? If so, should that condition be freedom at the end of military service as an inducement to the Negro to fight? Lastly, should the central government or the separate state governments take the problem in hand?

In Congress, Negro soldiery became the battleground over which Davis and his enemies were to fight for the last time. The President found that his friend

Hunter was "the chief obstacle" to the passage of the bill in the Senate, because it contained provision for manumission, or liberation from slavery, and the bill was indefinitely discussed, indefinitely put off. At this time a compromise bill was put through the House, but before it passed, its supporters again asked Lee for his sanction, which he again gave. Yet he was very explicit upon the question of state action, and it was doubtless his opinion that united all parties in the act of March 9, 1865. After more than two months of futile controversy, the act to arm the slaves empowered the President to ask for them, but that was all.

In these last terrifying months Davis had anticipated the law sanctioning the arming of the slaves by sending a secret emissary to Europe with power to promise abolition in exchange for intervention. This was the boldest step of his entire career, and as was the case with most of his plunges, it came too late. At last he had realized how powerful was the antislavery feeling in England. His plan was evidently to get the European powers to promise intervention and then to give the people a choice between intervention and success, without slavery, on the one hand, and failure, also without slavery, on the other.

Early in January, 1865, Duncan J. Kenner passed in disguise through the lines to New York, where he sailed for France. In Paris he held a conference with James Mason and John Slidell, and Mason at once went to England to announce what seemed to him an important decision to Lord Henry Palmerston. Mason reported that Palmerston was "conciliatory and kind" but denied that there was any unspoken reason for refusing recognition.

The North had been invaded too late; a cotton loan had been raised too late; the offensive in the West had been tried too late; Bragg was removed too late; Johnston was restored too late; the Negroes were armed too late; abolition of slavery was offered to Europe too late. And yet Davis was not directly responsible for all of these mistakes. Even the dispersive military system, in spite of the fact that he preferred it, was demanded by the feeling that underlied the doctrine of states' rights; every small community cried out for tangible protection day after day, regardless of disaster in main centers of war.

Now the President saw no one but by special appointment. Events were like a stone rolling from the crest of a mountain toward a cliff, steadily piling up momentum, till it reaches the brink and plunges to the abyss below. Davis was powerless to stop it. He could only look on with unseeing eyes. A pall was spreading over Richmond. Still the President, erect, dignified, walked through the Capitol Square. Mrs. Davis could barely serve a complete meal. Long ago she had sold her carriage horses, because she could not feed them on her husband's salary.

In the midst of the confusion of the last months the figure of Alexander H. Stephens appears for the last time, still nobly ignorant of reality, still convinced that

163

Davis was a monster, still devoted to a peace that he thought could be had for the mere asking. In January the peace movements of the summer of 1864 gathered in power.

Lincoln sent or permitted Francis P. Blair to go to Richmond on a peace mission. Blair proposed reunion and abolition and an expedition against Maximilian in Mexico to uphold the Monroe Doctrine, with Davis as the leader of the campaign. The Confederate House of Representatives was infatuated enough to hear to a bill approving the scheme. But Davis merely replied to Blair that he was willing to negotiate peace between the "two countries." The real purpose of Blair was to take the temperature of the Confederate leaders— which he found to be very low. So Lincoln's reply to Davis through Blair was that he was eager for peace in "our one common country." Jefferson Davis would not deceive himself with the belief that the North intended to let the South off short of utter subjugation; he knew it was either that or victory.

There were mutterings that Blair had offered attractive proposals, and Stephens, supposing that Davis was rejecting them because he wished to cling to his military tyranny, demanded that they be considered again. (It was an alarming autocracy that had been forced, quite futilely, to arm the slaves.) So Davis, utterly disillusioned, appointed Stephens, R. M. T. Hunter, and John A. Campbell as a commission to meet Lincoln and Seward in conference. On February 3, 1865, on a small steamboat in Hampton Roads, off Fortress

Monroe, the peacemakers talked for five or six hours—at the end of which Lincoln went away with the conviction that the war was nearly over. The Confederates had betrayed their despair. Hunter and Campbell would not consent to peace without victory; neither would Lincoln. Between the two views, the fantasy of Stephens, held with incredible ferocity for four years, collapsed. He returned to Richmond, wiser but not chastened, and ended his career as an unwilling Confederate by abandoning the government and going home to Georgia. The President had disposed of Stephens and his peacemakers only to put to the proof his own accurate judgment of the policy of the North and to confirm beyond hope his own despair.

But did he really despair? The grotesque failure of the peace conference forced upon all men the hard truth that they must fight or submit, and the determination to fight now hardened into something like mania in Jefferson Davis.

Toward the end of March, Davis told his wife that she and the children must leave Richmond and go to Charlotte, North Carolina. He gave her a pistol and showed her how to load, aim, and fire it. He said, "You can at least, if reduced to the last extremity, force your assailants to kill you, but I charge you solemnly to leave when the enemy are approaching. If you cannot remain undisturbed in our own country, make for the Florida coast and take a ship there for a foreign country."

Mrs. Davis did not want to be separated from him and pleaded to be allowed to stay, but he said his head-quarters might be in the field from now on, the presence of his family would only embarrass and grieve him, instead of comforting him. "If I live," he told her, "you can come to me when the struggle is ended, but I do not expect to survive the destruction of constitutional liberty."

He gave her a roll of Confederate bills and a small sum in gold, all the money he had except a five-dollar gold piece. Mrs. Davis hurriedly made her preparations for departure. The house was left just as it was—Davis would not even allow her to take along two barrels of flour which she had just bought. "You cannot remove anything in the shape of food from here," he said. "The people want it, and you must leave it here."

The trunks packed, Mrs. Davis, her children, and George A. Trenholm's daughters, were to set out on their journey under the escort of Burton Harrison. As they left the house, ten-year-old Maggie clung convulsively to her father while little Jeff said that he would not leave him. Davis' stern composure almost gave way for a moment. He stooped and gently put aside the children's clinging hands, then stood erect, composed for the leave-taking. He was convinced that he was looking his last upon his family; he did not expect to survive the Confederacy.

Lee's army, starving and in rags while warehouses full of clothing and supplies of food lay at the far ends of broken railways, was now reduced to 30,000 men holding a line thirty miles long. Grant faced them with 120,000.

April 2 was Sunday, and the President went in the morning to Saint Paul's Church. Dr. Minnigerode was delivering his sermon. A messenger came in and handed Jefferson Davis a piece of paper. It was a telegram from Lee. It said that Grant had broken the Confederate line at Five Forks, that Richmond must be evacuated. The rumor was not unwarranted. The President quietly and deliberately rose and, with perhaps only a slightly quickened step, left the church.

9 Flight

ALL SUNDAY AFTERNOON President Davis collected and aranged his papers, having sent word to his Cabinet officers that the government would leave at the earliest possible moment for Danville, Virginia, toward which town Lee was retreating, with Grant close upon his track.

Throughout the afternoon, wagons drawn by gaunt horses and mules rumbled along the cobbled streets, toward the bridges leading to the Southwest. Men on horseback galloped furiously to and fro. A long procession of weary-looking people, carrying bundles of every size, steadily poured over the bridges into the town of Manchester and into the open country beyond.

At dawn of April 3, three of the great bridges over the James were in flames; warehouses and factories on the banks of the river, now on fire, were crumbling to ashes. At short, irregular intervals, magazines ex-

169

ploded, throwing bricks and dust into the air; piles of cartridges caught fire, rattling and crackling like a great battle, in the midst of the seething hiss of the fires rapidly sweeping away the lower part of the city.

At the one remaining bridge a small guard stood ready with pine firebrands—the last of the defenders of the city. A long wagon train dashed at a gallop down the street and over the bridge. The guard still waited. A heavy column of Confederate cavalry swung out of a side street toward the bridge and clattered across to the other side of the river. The guard set the bridge on fire and followed.

In the distance, on the south side of the river, the last Confederates disappeared over the crest of a hill just as a squad of blue horsemen rode down Main Street in pursuit. The Federals halted before the burning bridge. Other squads filled the streets. Then dense masses of Union infantry, their bayonets glistening through the smoke, marched through the streets, without end. Wild cheers burst forth as they reached Capitol Square. Richmond, after four years of bloody war, had fallen at last.

By nightfall Union General Weitzel had got the mobs and fires under control and began issuing rations to the famished people.

The next day, April 4, a tall, bony man wearing a long black cape and a stovepipe hat, followed by a squad of Marines, walked along East Clay Street. His gait shambling but alert, he gazed with intense curiosity at everything around him. Meeting a Union officer, he asked, "Is it far to President Davis' house?" He was told that it was only a few minutes away. The tall man passed on. He came to the house, now the headquarters of General Weitzel, and went in. As he sat down in Jefferson Davis' office, he said, "This must have been President Davis' chair." Then, crossing his legs, he looked abstractedly into space. Suddenly he looked up and inquired if the housekeeper were in. She was not in. "Come," he said, "let's look at the house!" He looked at all the rooms, even the bedrooms, with child-like curiosity, while an officer told him gossip that he had picked up from the housekeeper. General Weitzel arrived, and Abraham Lincoln grew serious again.

The capital had fallen, but in the opinion of Jefferson Davis, the Confederacy had not. After a slow trip on the crippled Richmond and Danville Railroad, the Confederate Government arrived in Danville on April 3. The Cabinet members found quarters where they could, but the President was received in the home of a Mr. and Mrs. Sutherlin, where he remained for a week. In this time he anxiously looked around for offices suitable for the temporarily dispossessed government, for it was his intention to keep the capital of the Confederate states, if possible, on Virginia soil.

A strange calm had come over him since he had left Richmond, a certain blind optimism at the lowest ebb of his career—a proud and unyielding confidence that, in spite of the catastrophe surrounding him, he was now about to succeed.

171

No news of Lee reached Danville. On day at the dinner table, Davis' hostess asked, "Mr. Davis, would Lee's surrender end the war?"

"By no means," he replied. "We'll fight it out to the Mississippi River." Some of the Cabinet officers agreed to this.

The days passed, and the President had never seemed so poised or so self-confident. It was only a matter of time . . . a matter of time. He would fight to the end, beyond the end.

The days passed, and one morning a haggard youth arrived in Danville, dressed in a seedy-looking Confederate officer's uniform and riding a broken-down horse. He asked for President Davis.

Davis and Sutherlin came excitedly into the Sutherlin house. Mrs. Sutherlin met them at the door, and the President said in a low tone, almost a whisper, "Lee has surrendered. I must leave Danville immediately."

Within a few minutes he had gathered up his baggage and was ready to go. Then he shook hands with Mrs. Sutherlin. "Mr. Davis," she asked, "have you any funds other than Confederate money?"

He answered no.

"Then," Mrs. Sutherlin replied, "you must take this from me." She held out a bag containing $2,000 in gold.

He took the lady's hand again, tears in his eyes.

"No, I cannot take your money. You and your husband are young and will need your money, while I am an old man." (He was only fifty-six.) After a pause, he added, "I don't reckon I shall need anything very long."

He reached into his pocket and took out a small gold pencil. Giving it to Mrs. Sutherlin, he asked her to take it as a keepsake. Then he turned and walked away to the train. The cars were loaded with Cabinet officers, members of the Presidential staff, hangers-on, their families. The train started for Greensboro, North Carolina.

At Greensboro the Confederate Government made its headquarters at the residence of Colonel John Taylor Wood, where the Cabinet met for the last time. In an upstairs bedroom all the members who remained were present—Mallory, Benjamin, Reagan, General Breckinridge, the last Secretary of War, and staff officers. The room contained a bed, some small chairs, a table with pen and ink. Presently there was a knock at the door.

General Johnston and General Beauregard entered, and after some casual talk, the conference began. The President surveyed the gathering with a calm, unhurried eye and seemed unmoved by the strangeness of his situation. He began with some remarks having no relation to the critical moment. He still seemed to see himself as the head of a powerful government, backed by immense resources, perfectly secure, unpressed by time.

At last he looked at General Johnston and said, "Our late disasters have been terrible, but I do not think we should regard them as fatal. I think we can whip the enemy yet if our people turn out. . . . Whatever can be done must be done at once. We have not a day to lose."

Johnston said nothing, and finally the President said, "We should like to hear your views, General Johnston."

The general spoke quickly, intensely, as if he were in anger. "My views are, sir, that our people are tired of the war, feel themselves whipped, and will not fight. . . . We cannot place another large army in the field. . . . My men are daily deserting in large numbers. . . . Since Lee's defeat they regarded the war at an end. . . . I shall expect to retain no man beyond the byroad or cowpath that leads to his house. . . . We may perhaps obtain terms that we ought to accept."

During this speech, Davis sat with his eyes fixed upon a scrap of paper on the table before him, which he was folding and refolding with careful abstraction even after Johnston had ceased. He suddenly looked at Beauregard. "What do you say, General Beauregard?" His voice was low and measured.

Beauregard replied, "I concur in all General Johnston has said."

It was agreed that a letter should be written to Sherman asking for terms, and Johnston asked the President to write it—which he did. The meeting broke up.

On April 16 the Confederate Government took to the road to go farther south. The President and his staff and most of the fast dwindling Cabinet rode their horses, but in the rear an ambulance bore the Secretary of State, Benjamin, his brother-in-law, De Saint-Martin, General Samuel Cooper, and George Davis, the Attorney General. The column moved day and night toward Charlotte—where the President hoped to find his wife and children—but the progress was slow, almost aimless, in spite of the President's desire to join the army in the Trans-Mississippi Department.

At Charlotte, Davis found that his wife had gone to South Carolina, so he sent Harrison after her, to Abbeville, to arrange a place of meeting. The government was now somewhat unpopular; only with great difficulty could the party find lodgings. Stoneman's Federal cavalry had threatened to burn every house that received Jefferson Davis. In a few days a message arrived announcing the murder of President Lincoln, and the whole party expressed regret and surprise. Davis said to Colonel William Preston Johnston, "Mr. Lincoln would have been more useful to the Southern states than Andrew Johnson, his successor, is likely to be." At Charlotte, he made a speech—his last as President—to some troopers of General Basil Duke's cavalry, but he made not the slightest allusion to the death of Lincoln. He had no sympathy with whomever had committed the crime—the details of which at that time he did not know.

In Charlotte the President was extremely cheerful and agreeable. He had probably never been so amiable before. He talked freely, but with the ordinary restraint of a man enjoying casual social intercourse. No violent opinions escaped him. He was a revolutionist who had not flouted a single convention of either private or public morality, who had made war with rigid propriety, according to the strictest rules, who had taken to none of the extreme measures that, if followed by success, his position would have justified. He could say, indeed, that his enemy, not he, had violated the rules of "chivalric warfare." And he could say, as he actually did say at Charlotte, what was true of all men of honor in whatever circumstances: "I cannot feel like a beaten man."

An armistice between Johnston and Sherman came to an end on April 24, because the Federal Government would not ratify it. Shereman, having conquered the South, was willing to let the Southern states quietly resume their place in the Union, but his superiors denied his right to treat political question. When Davis heard this, he left Charlotte and began his slow, almost leisurely march through South Carolina. Two members of his Cabinet had disappeared, but all his staff was there, and at his back rode about 2,000 cavalry. More than a week passed, and at last on May 4 the Confederate Government crossed the Savannah River into Georgia. At a house along the road some people were kind to the President, so he gave them his last coin—a five-dollar gold piece.

At Washington, Georgia, the President, lodging in the home of a Dr. Robinson, formally disbanded his

Cabinet. He had heard of Johnston's surrender, which had taken place on April 26, and he knew now that there was no further chance of resistance or of getting agreeable terms from the Federal Government. The Union had definitely won a complete conquest of the South.

Federal cavalry were in close pursuit, and the people in the village of Washington urged the President to leave. At midnight some of the Cabinet officers and others of the party took to the roads. Next morning, Davis was expected to leave at an early hour. He appeared to be not in the least hurried. He was informed that Mrs. Davis was awaiting him at Raytown, but he had to speak to the ladies who had called. He was informed that his horse was at the door, but he had to kiss the little children who were present. He stood beside his horse, pausing to receive the good wishes and encouragement of one of his hosts. He said, " 'Though He slay me, yet will I trust Him.' "

Then he mounted his horse, very slowly, "and, Colonel Johnston doing the same, the two passed out of the town with the painful slowness of mourners in a funeral procession . . . think of the high bearing, the granite firmness of the man. . . ."

For two days the President and his small mounted escort—the body of cavalry having dropped off— pushed farther toward the south till news came that a band of ruffians, stragglers or paroled men, men of both armies, were pursuing his family; so he turned to the east, hoping to find them. One nightfall the horses of his guard broke down, but he pressed on with only his personal staff.

The night was brilliantly moonlit, and just as the moon sank behind the trees a voice hailed the president's party. He himself answered and was greeted by Burton Harrison, who immediately took him to his family near the village of Irwinsville in Georgia. He rode along with his family for several days, but on the evening of May 10 he saddled his horse, inspected his pistols, and got ready to leave. One of his staff suddenly brought him news that marauders intended to attack the camp that night, so he decided to wait until the alarm had passed He lay down, fully dressed, in the tent. Harrison fell asleep outside on the ground. So the night passed.

At dawn, Jim Jones, the freed Negro coachman who had followed Mrs. Davis from Richmond, woke the whole camp with shouts that the enemy was upon them!

There was a crackle of rifle fire. Harrison jumped to his feet and saw a blue regiment, which was the Fourth Michigan Cavalry, charging up the road from the direction opposite the firing. In a moment Colonel Johnston was taken prisoner, and then Colonel Pritchard, the Union commander, halting his men, rode directly to Harrison and demanded as he pointed across the creek from which the firing had come, "What does this mean? Have you any men with you?"

"Of course, we have," said Harrison. "Don't you hear the firing?"

The Yankee seemed taken aback, so he ordered his men to charge toward the firing—which had come from other Federals across the creek. Meanwhile, the camp was deserted but for one Union trooper standing in front of the President's tent and a few who were lost in pillage of the wagons.

At the sound of the alarm the President rose. "I hope I still have influence enough with the Confederates to prevent your being robbed," he said to his wife. Then he looked outside and saw the blue uniforms. Not wishing to leave Mrs. Davis alone, he hesitated. His horse and pistols were in the road now held by the enemy; he could not reach them. He picked up a light rainproof coat, a raglan, and put it on; it was his wife's, but so nearly like his own that he took it. Mrs. Davis now urged him to get away. As he started out, she threw a shawl over his head to protect him from the dampness of early morning.

But Mrs. Davis went out first, saying something to the mounted man stationed at her tent. Harrison, being quick-witted, ran swiftly up to the soldier and, after a few words, actually persuaded him to go away, walking at the side of his horse down the road. The President suddenly came out of the far side of the tent and walked rapidly toward the woods, not glancing back.

The soldier whom Harrison had tricked looked around and, seeing that someone had left the tent, turned his horse back to the spot where he had been a moment before. Two other troopers joined him and began speaking harshly and abusively to Mrs. Davis.

The President, now about twenty yards away, over-hearing the abuse, seemed to hesitate but continued toward the woods. One of the soldiers saw him, and shouted, "Halt!"

The order was not obeyed. The man yelled again, "Halt!" and repeated it; still he was not obeyed. Then he raised his carbine and threatened to fire.

Mrs. Davis shrieked and ran after her husband, who turned sharply and began walking quickly back to the tent. He immediately reproached the soldiers for using ungentlemanly language to his wife.

"Mr. Davis, surrender! I recognize you, sir!"

The pillage began. Mrs. Davis' trunks were broken open, and a new hoopskirt taken out. A soldier, forcing open a trunk with the barrel of his carbine, shot off his own hand. After an hour, the captives were started back toward Macon, toward Augusta, toward the casements of Fortress Monroe. The soldiers called Mr. Davis Jeff.

It was said that Jefferson Davis had on his wife's hoopskirt when he was captured—trying to escape in disguise. Thousands believed it then, and doubtless thousands believe it still.

10 Epilogue

So JEFFERSON DAVIS and the Southern Confederacy fell. And yet the leader of the Lost Cause
lived on until 1889, proud to the end and never moving an inch from his convictions of 1861. His post-
bellum life was an existence, not a career, and at times,
in the terrors of Reconstruction, it was meager. The
chronic neurotic of the sixties turned, as the years
passed, into the fatherly maker of speeches at the lay-
ings of cornerstones, at the dedications of monuments,
at religious meetings. He was presented with a comfortable home on the Gulf of Mexico, and he grew just
a little fat. The fierce passions of his prime cooled to
the gentle wisdom of the patriarch. He wrote letters
and histories of the war, refuted slanders, argued with
Joseph E. Johnston, visited England and France,
snubbed Louis Napoleon for his doublehanded policy
with the South, came home and received, at last, the

adoration of his people. He was the "President" until he died.

He deserved to be; he had lain in Fortress Monroe, charged with treason, for two years, much of the time in chains, separated from his family and his friends. He became the sacrifice of the Southern people to the passions of the Northern mobs, whose leaders could hardly have let him off without a show of punishment. The lust of the crowd had to be appeased.

Yet the Federal Government knew not what to do with him. If he was a traitor, why was he not hanged? He was not even tried, although there were legal mummeries that were carefully gone through, and the crowd was pleased that a grand jury partly composed of Negroes was impaneled to indict him. The Federal Government did not wish to try him. It could not run the risk of having its charge of treason turned into a legal vindication of secession, for such would probably have been the issue. The Federal Government would have felt just a little ridiculous to have had set aside by a court what it had won by the sword. It was satisfied to take its victory and, as soon as a few minor hangings were accomplished, to let Jefferson Davis go.

From 1865 to 1889—twenty-four years of anticlimax, of death in life. Jefferson Davis died on May 11, 1865.

What was the war about? That, in this story, has not been our great concern. Davis and Stephens believed that it was fought by the South for constitutional liberty, and this was doubtless right; this was one way of saying it, because, politically, that was the South's defense. R. M. T. Hunter of Virginia and William Lloyd Garrison of Massachusetts believed that slavery was the cause of the War Between the States—Hunter fought to protect slavery; Garrison to destroy it—and yet both of these slightly unphilosophical gentlemen were profoundly wrong. The North's real interest in abolishing slavery was in all respects identical with the interest of the United States in 1917 in making the world safe for democracy. In 1816 the tariff issue became acute, and within five years Abolitionist societies were gathering in the North. The relation between these two interesting phenomena may be a subject of dispute, but at the same time it is an object of suspicion.

The War Between the States has a remote origin, and it cannot be understood apart from the chief movements of European history since the Reformation. It was another war between America and Europe, and America, in the second great attempt, won. The South was the last stronghold of European civilization in the Western Hemisphere, a conservative check upon the restless expansiveness of the industrial North, and the South had to go. The South was permanently old-fashioned, backward-looking, slow, contented to live upon a modest conquest of nature, unwilling to conquer the earth's resources for the fun of the conquest— contented, in short, to take only what man needs, unwilling to juggle the needs of man in the illusory pursuit of abstract wealth. It is a mistake to suppose that the surrender of Lord Cornwallis at Yorktown in 1781 freed America from the bonds of the European tradition; that somewhat mottled blessing required for its success one more surrender—that of Lee at Appomattox in 1865. The War Between the States was the second and decisive struggle of the Western spirit against the European—the spirit of restless aggression against a stable spirit of ordered economy—and the Western won.

In a sense, all European history since the Reformation was concentrated in the war between the North and the South. For in the South the most conservative of the European orders had, with great power, come back to life; while in the North, opposing the Southern feudalism, there had grown a powerful industrial state which epitomized in spirit all those middle-class, urban impulses directed against the agrarian aristocracies of Europe after the Reformation. The transformation of Europe, its Americanization within Europe, has been gradual, but the transformation of Europe in America was, because its two spiritual poles clashed here, sudden and dramatic.

The critical period in America arrived in about 1830. The New England industrial system, although at first conservative and patriarchal, contained the seed of the Western spirit, and by 1840 its growth in the East was sufficiently rank to begin choking out those ways of feeling and living that New England no less than the South had inherited from Europe. The conquest of heaven became, without much abating its zeal, the conquest of brute nature—and in the end, as it often happens, the conqueror capitulated to the enemy.

However, as we have seen, the old agrarianism did not fall without a struggle. From April 2 to 9, 1865, the men who had seen what was coming and had decided that they might as well fight as be smothered were sadly reduced, but they were not willing, the handful that still hung on, to quit. The army that had never been beaten on the field, that had beaten its enemy time and again, was not beaten at last. It simply collapsed.

Index

187

The Author

Allen Tate, the noted American critic and historian, has published more than a score of books. This biography of Jefferson Davis stems from his deep interest in the Confederate leader, about whom he wrote a widely acclaimed study several years ago. Mr. Tate, who was graduated from Vanderbilt University in Nashville, Tennessee, has been a Fulbright professor at Oxford and taught and lectured at many American universities, most recently at the University of Minnesota. At present he and his wife live in Sewanee, Tennessee.